Academic

Preparation

In English

**Teaching for Transition
From High School
To College**

D0777982

College Entrance Examination Board, New York, 1985

Academic Preparation in English is one of a series of six books. The Academic Preparation Series includes books in English, the Arts, Mathematics, Science, Social Studies, and Foreign Language. Single copies of any one of these books can be purchased for $6.95. Orders for 5 to 49 copies receive a 20% discount; orders for 50 or more receive a 50% discount.

A boxed set of all the books in the Academic Preparation Series is available for $20.00. Orders for five or more sets receive a 20% discount. Each set also includes a copy of *Academic Preparation for College: What Students Need to Know and Be Able to Do.*

Payment or purchase order for individual titles or the set should be addressed to: College Board Publications, Box 886, New York, New York 10101.

The poem "Harlem" on page 49 is reprinted by permission. Copyright © 1951 by Langston Hughes. Originally published in *The Panther and the Lash*, in *Selected Poems of Langston Hughes* (New York: Alfred A. Knopf, 1959), page 199.

The poem "The Death of a Toad" on pages 52-53 is reprinted by permission. Copyright © 1950, 1978 by Richard Wilbur. Originally published in *Ceremony and Other Poems*, by Richard Wilbur, in 1950. Taken from *The Poems of Richard Wilbur* (New York: Harcourt, Brace & World, 1967), page 152.

The excerpt from "The Kitchen," in *A Walker in the City*, which appears in Appendix A and in a shortened version on page 66, is reprinted by permission. Copyright © 1951, 1979 by Alfred Kazin. Alfred Kazin, *A Walker in the City* (New York and London: Harcourt Brace Jovanovich, 1951), pages 64-71.

9 8 7 6 5 4 3

Contents

Principal Consultant

Edward. R. Ducharme, Professor of Education and Chairman of Organizational Counseling and Foundational Studies, University of Vermont, Burlington

English Advisory Committee, 1984-85

Jan A. Guffin, North Central High School, Indianapolis, Indiana (*Chair*)

Roger K. Applebee, College of Liberal Arts and Sciences, University of Illinois at Urbana-Champaign, Urbana

Michael C. Flanigan, University of Oklahoma, Norman

Ann L. Hayes, Carnegie-Mellon University, Pittsburgh, Pennsylvania

Raul S. Murguia, The High Technology High School at San Antonio College, Texas

Emma M. Ruff, New Haven Public Schools, Connecticut

Jane C. Schaffer, Santana High School, Santee, California

Acknowledgments

The College Board wishes to thank all the individuals and organizations that contributed to *Academic Preparation in English*. In addition to those who served on the English Advisory Committee and the Council on Academic Affairs, explicit acknowledgment should be accorded to Robert Orrill, Barbara Martinsons, Yola Coffeen, Mary Carroll Scott, and Carol J. Meyer. Without the leadership of Adrienne Y. Bailey, vice president for Academic Affairs at the College Board, this book would not have assumed its present form. Although none of these people is individually responsible for the contents of the book, the Educational EQuality Project owes much to their efforts.

James Herbert, General Editor

The College Board is a nonprofit membership organization that provides tests and other educational services for students, schools, and colleges. The membership is composed of more than 2,500 colleges, schools, school systems, and education associations. Representatives of the members serve on the Board of Trustees and advisory councils and committees that consider the College Board's programs and participate in the determination of its policies and activities.

The Educational EQuality Project is a 10-year effort of the College Board to strengthen the academic quality of secondary education and to ensure equality of opportunity for postsecondary education for all students. Begun in 1980, the project is under the direction of the Board's Office of Academic Affairs.

For more information about the Educational EQuality Project and inquiries about this report, write to the Office of Academic Affairs, The College Board, 45 Columbus Avenue, New York, New York 10023-6917.

To Our Fellow Teachers of English

This book is the work, not of one teacher, but of many. As a result it contains the sound of several voices and traces of different hands. In bringing it to completion we thought at first to replace this variety with a single manner and tone but, in the end, realized that doing so would result in a deep inconsistency and detract from our purpose. What we want, after all, is for English teachers to join in the discussion we have begun, adding their own thoughts to ours and fitting the ideas to local situations. Since the book itself is the product of exactly this kind of collaboration, we believe that it is appropriate and perhaps useful to retain the signs of varied contribution. Their presence indicates the active participation that made the book and that we hope to encourage in our readers.

However, in matters of approach and substance we are in agreement—even though there is much that we do not know for certain about language. Does language precede thought? Or does thinking come before talking? Or does syntax exist before either? Such questions, we believe, reveal that the study of language is a search into one of life's profound mysteries. To use language is to tap a great source of power. Our goal as English teachers is to help students use this power effectively and to respect it as one would any natural force.

We believe that we have taught well over the years, particularly those bright, imaginative, and ambitious students who are eager to do well—the ones perhaps who remind us of ourselves. With this group of students, we feel good about our efforts and take pride in the results. But what of other students? How do we do with the vast majority of high school students? Many of them go on to higher education, and many do not; the research does not show us why. But if we believe, as we do, that teachers make some difference in the life choices young people make, then we should strive to do better with these students. Maybe *we* are the variable. We should better prepare the ones who will go on to college so that they can do better work, and better prepare those who might otherwise not go so that they have wider choices and opportunities. Justice in a free society demands that we do so.

Perhaps we have taught some students facts but not how to understand them, the elements of "correct" prose rather than the achievement of it, and the rudiments of middle-class spoken English without a synthesis of it into their broader language repertoire. Perhaps we have not believed these students capable of the level of performance required for understanding, achievement, and synthesis. If so, we underestimate the potential of many young Americans.

The following chapters are one voice in what we think of as a dialogue—a dialogue of hope and vision. We believe that, with consensus on some basic issues, we can do much better with all our students and that we can provide them with opportunities to learn and achieve that will, in turn, help open the world of possibilities that exists in college and in the rest of the broader society beyond high school.

English Advisory Committee

I. Beyond the Green Book

Identifying the academic preparation needed for college is a first step toward providing that preparation for all students who might aspire to higher education. But the real work of actually achieving these learning outcomes lies ahead.[1]

This book is a sequel to *Academic Preparation for College: What Students Need to Know and Be Able to Do,* which was published in 1983 by the College Board's Educational EQuality Project. Now widely known as the Green Book, *Academic Preparation for College* outlined the knowledge and skills students need in order to have a fair chance at succeeding in college. It summarized the combined judgments of hundreds of educators in every part of the country. The Green Book sketched learning outcomes that could serve as goals for high school curricula in six Basic Academic Subjects: English, the arts, mathematics, science, social studies, and foreign languages. It also identified six Basic Academic Competencies on which depend, and which are further developed by, work in these subjects. Those competencies are reading, writing, speaking and listening, mathematics, reasoning, and studying. The Green Book also called attention to additional competencies in using computers and observing, whose value to the college entrant increasingly is being appreciated.

With this book we take a step beyond *Academic Preparation for College.* The Green Book simply outlined desired results of high school education—the learning all students need to be adequately prepared for college. It contained no specific suggestions about how to achieve those results. Those of us working with the Educational EQuality Project strongly believed—and still believe—that ultimately curriculum and instruction are matters of local expertise

---

1. The College Board, *Academic Preparation for College: What Students Need to Know and Be Able to Do* (New York: The College Board, 1983), p. 31.

and responsibility. Building consensus on goals, while leaving flexible the means to achieve them, makes the most of educators' ability to respond appropriately and creatively to conditions in their own schools. Nevertheless, teachers and administrators, particularly those closely associated with the EQuality project, often have asked how the outcomes sketched in the Green Book might be translated into actual curricula and instructional practices—how they can get on with the "real work" of education. These requests in part seek suggestions about how the Green Book goals might be achieved; perhaps to an even greater extent they express a desire to get a fuller picture of those very briefly stated goals. Educators prefer to think realistically, in terms of courses and lessons. Discussion of proposals such as those in the Green Book proceeds more readily when goals are filled out and cast into the practical language of possible courses of action.

To respond to these requests for greater detail, and to encourage further nationwide discussion about what should be happening in our high school classrooms, teachers working with the Educational EQuality Project have prepared this book and five like it, one in each of the Basic Academic Subjects. By providing suggestions about how the outcomes described in *Academic Preparation for College* might be achieved, we hope to add more color and texture to the sketches in that earlier publication. We do not mean these suggestions to be prescriptive or definitive, but to spark more detailed discussion and ongoing dialogue among our fellow teachers who have the front-line responsibility for ensuring that all students are prepared adequately for college. We also intend this book and its companions for guidance counselors, principals, superintendents, and other officials who must understand the work of high school teachers if they are better to support and cooperate with them.

Students at Risk, Nation at Risk

Academic Preparation for College was the result of an extensive grassroots effort involving hundreds of educators in every part of the country. However, it was not published in a vacuum. Since the beginning of this decade, many blue-ribbon commissions and stud-

4

ies also have focused attention on secondary education. The concerns of these reports have been twofold. One, the reports note a perceptible decline in the academic attainments of students who graduate from high school, as indicated by such means as standardized test scores and comments from employers; two, the reports reflect a widespread worry that, unless students are better educated, our national welfare will be in jeopardy. *A Nation at Risk* made this point quite bluntly:

> Our Nation is at risk. Our once unchallenged preeminence in commerce, industry, science, and technological innovation is being overtaken by competitors throughout the world. . . . The educational foundations of our society are presently being eroded by a rising tide of mediocrity that threatens our very future as a Nation and a people.[2]

The Educational EQuality Project, an effort of the College Board throughout the decade of the 1980s to improve both the quality of preparation for college and the equality of access to it, sees another aspect of risk: if our nation is at risk because of the level of students' educational attainment, then we must be more concerned with those students who have been most at risk.

Overall, the predominance of the young in our society is ending. In 1981, as the EQuality project was getting under way, about 41 percent of our country's population was under 25 years old and 26 percent was 50 years old or older. By the year 2000, however, the balance will have shifted to 34 percent and 28 percent, respectively. But these figures do not tell the whole story, especially for those of us working in the schools. Among certain groups, youth is a growing segment of the population. For example, in 1981, 71 percent of black and 75 percent of Hispanic households had children 18 years old or younger. In comparison, only 52 percent of all white households had children in that age category. At the beginning of the 1980s, children from minority groups already made up more than 25 percent of all public school students.[3] Clearly, concern for im-

---

2. National Commission on Excellence in Education, *A Nation at Risk* (Washington, D.C.: U.S. Government Printing Office, 1983), p. 5.

3. Ernest L. Boyer, *High School* (New York: Harper & Row, 1983), pp. 4-5. U.S. Department of Education, National Center for Education Statistics, *Digest of Education Statistics: 1982* (Washington, D.C.: U.S. Government Printing Office, 1982), p. 43.

proving the educational attainments of all students increasingly must involve concern for students from such groups of historically disadvantaged Americans.

How well will such young people be educated? In a careful and thoughtful study of schools, John Goodlad found that "consistent with the findings of virtually every study that has considered the distribution of poor and minority students . . . minority students were found in disproportionately large percentages in the low track classes of the multiracial samples [of the schools studied]."[4] The teaching and learning that occur in many such courses can be disappointing in comparison to that occurring in other courses. Goodlad reported that in many such courses very little is expected, and very little is attempted.[5]

When such students are at risk, the nation itself is at risk, not only economically but morally. That is why this book and its five companions offer suggestions that will be useful in achieving academic excellence for *all* students. We have attempted to take into account that the resources of some high schools may be limited and that some beginning high school students may not be well prepared. We have tried to identify ways to keep open the option of preparing adequately for college as late as possible in the high school years. These books are intended for work with the broad spectrum of high school students—not just a few students and not only those currently in the "academic track." We are convinced that many more students can—and, in justice, should—profit from higher education and therefore from adequate academic preparation.

Moreover, many more students actually enroll in postsecondary education than currently follow the "academic track" in high school. Further, discussions with employers have emphasized that many of the same academic competencies needed by college-bound students also are needed by high school students going directly into the world of work. Consequently, the Educational EQuality Project, as its name indicates, hopes to contribute to achieving a democratic excellence in our high schools.

---

4. John Goodlad, *A Place Called School* (New York: McGraw-Hill, 1984), p. 156.

5. Ibid., p. 159.

The Classroom: At the Beginning as Well as the End of Improvement

A small book such as this one, intended only to stimulate dialogue about what happens in the classroom, cannot address all the problems of secondary education. On the other hand, we believe that teachers and the actual work of education—that is to say, curriculum and instruction—should be a more prominent part of the nationwide discussion about improving secondary education.

A 1984 report by the Education Commission of the States found that 44 states either had raised high school graduation requirements or had such changes pending. Twenty-seven states had enacted new policies dealing with instructional time, such as new extracurricular policies and reduced class sizes.[6] This activity reflects the momentum for and concern about reform that has been generated recently. It demonstrates a widespread recognition that critiques of education without concrete proposals for change will not serve the cause of improvement. But what will such changes actually mean in the classroom? New course requirements do not necessarily deal with the academic quality of the courses used to fulfill those requirements. Certain other kinds of requirements can force instruction to focus on the rote acquisition of information to the exclusion of fuller intellectual development. Manifestly, juggling of requirements and courses without attention to what needs to occur between teachers and students inside the classroom will not automatically produce better prepared students. One proponent of reform, Ernest Boyer, has noted that there is danger in the prevalence of "quick-fix" responses to the call for improvement. "The depth of discussion about the curriculum . . . has not led to a serious and creative look at the nature of the curriculum. . . . states [have not asked] what we ought to be teaching."[7]

Such questioning and discussion is overdue. Clearly, many im-

---

6. *Action in the States: Progress toward Education Renewal*, A Report by the Task Force on Education for Economic Growth (Denver, Colorado: Education Commission of the States, 1984), p. 27.

7. In Thomas Toch, "For School Reform's Top Salesmen, It's Been Some Year," *Education Week*, June 6, 1984, p. 33.

provements in secondary education require action outside the class-room and the school. Equally clearly, even this action should be geared to a richer, more developed understanding of what is needed in the classroom. By publishing these books we hope to add balance to the national debate about improving high school education. Our point is not only that it is what happens between teachers and students in the classroom that makes the difference. Our point is also that what teachers and students do in classrooms must be thoughtfully considered before many kinds of changes, even exterior changes, are made in the name of educational improvement.

From Deficit to Development

What we can do in the classroom is limited, of course, by other factors. Students must be there to benefit from what happens in class. Teachers know firsthand that far too many young people of high school age are no longer even enrolled. Nationally, the drop-out rate in 1980 among the high school population aged 14 to 34 was 13 percent. It was higher among low-income and minority students. Nearly 1 out of 10 high schools had a drop-out rate of over 20 percent.[8]

Even when students stay in high school, we know that they do not always have access to the academic preparation they need. Many do not take enough of the right kinds of courses. In 1980, in almost half of all high schools, a majority of the students in each of those schools was enrolled in the "general" curriculum. Nation-wide, only 38 percent of high school seniors had been in an academic program; another 36 percent had been in a general program; and 24 percent had followed a vocational/technical track. Only 39 percent of these seniors had enrolled for three or more years in history or social studies; only 33 percent had taken three or more years of mathematics; barely 22 percent had taken three or more

---

8. National Center for Education Statistics, *Digest of Education Statistics: 1982*, p. 68. Donald A. Rock, et al., "Factors Associated with Test Score Decline: Briefing Paper" (Princeton, New Jersey: Educational Testing Service, December 1984), p. 4.

years of science; and less than 8 percent of these students had studied Spanish, French, or German for three or more years.[9]

Better than anyone else, teachers know that, even when students are in high school and are enrolled in the needed academic courses, they must attend class regularly. Yet some school systems report daily absence rates as high as 20 percent. When 1 out of 5 students enrolled in a course is not actually there, it is difficult even to begin carrying out a sustained, coherent program of academic preparation.

As teachers we know that such problems cannot be solved solely by our efforts in the classroom. In a world of disrupted family and community structures; economic hardship; and rising teenage pregnancy, alcoholism, and suicide, it would be foolish to believe that attention to curriculum and instruction can remedy all the problems leading to students' leaving high school, taking the wrong courses, and missing classes. Nonetheless, what happens in the high school classroom—once students are there—is important in preparing students not only for further education but for life.

Moreover, as teachers, we also hope that what happens in the classroom at least can help students stick with their academic work. Students may be increasingly receptive to this view. In 1980 more than 70 percent of high school seniors wanted greater academic emphasis in their schools; this was true of students in all curricula. Mortimer Adler may have described a great opportunity:

> There is little joy in most of the learning they [students] are now compelled to do. Too much of it is make-believe, in which neither teacher nor pupil can take a lively interest. Without some joy in learning—a joy that arises from hard work well done and from the participation of one's mind in a common task—basic schooling cannot initiate the young into the life of learning, let alone give them the skill and the incentive to engage in it further.[10]

Genuine academic work can contribute to student motivation and persistence. Goodlad's study argues strongly that the widespread

---

9. National Center for Education Statistics, *Digest of Education Statistics: 1982*, p. 70.

10. Mortimer J. Adler, *The Paideia Proposal: An Educational Manifesto* (New York: Macmillan Publishing Company, 1982), p. 32.

focus on the rote mechanics of a subject is a surefire way to distance students from it or to ensure that they do not comprehend all that they are capable of understanding. Students need to be encouraged to become inquiring, involved learners. It is worth trying to find more and better ways to engage them actively in the learning process, to build on their strengths and enthusiasms. Consequently, the approaches suggested in these books try to shift attention from chronicling what students do not know toward developing the full intellectual attainments of which they are capable and which they will need in college.

Dimensions for a Continuing Dialogue

This book and its five companions were prepared during 1984 and 1985 under the aegis of the College Board's Academic Advisory Committees. Although each committee focused on the particular issues facing its subject, the committees had common purposes and common approaches. Those purposes and approaches may help give shape to the discussion that this book and its companions hope to stimulate.

Each committee sought the assistance of distinguished writers and consultants. The committees considered suggestions made in the dialogues that preceded and contributed to *Academic Preparation for College* and called on guest colleagues for further suggestions and insights. Each committee tried to take account of the best available thinking and research but did not merely pass along the results of research or experience. Each deliberated about those findings and then tried to suggest approaches that had actually worked to achieve learning outcomes described in *Academic Preparation for College*. The suggestions in these books are based to a great extent on actual, successful high school programs.

These books focus not only on achieving the outcomes for a particular subject described in the Green Book but also on how study of that subject can develop the Basic Academic Competencies. The learning special to each subject has a central role to play in preparing students for successful work in college. That role ought not to be neglected in a rush to equip students with more general skills. It is learning in a subject that can engage a student's interest, activity, and commitment. Students do, after all, read about *something*, write about *something*, reason about *something*. We thought it important to suggest that developing the Basic Academic Competencies does not replace, but can result from, mastering the unique knowledge and skills of each Basic Academic Subject. Students, particularly hungry and undernourished ones, should not be asked to master the use of the fork, knife, and spoon without being served an appetizing, full, and nourishing meal.

In preparing the book for each subject, we also tried to keep in mind the connections among the Basic Academic Subjects. For example, the teaching of English and the other languages should build on students' natural linguistic appetite and development—and this lesson may apply to the teaching of other subjects as well. The teaching of history with emphasis on the full range of human experience, as approached through both social and global history, bears on the issue of broadening the "canon" of respected works in literature and the arts. The teaching of social studies, like the teaching of science, involves mathematics not only as a tool but as a mode of thought. There is much more to make explicit and to explore in such connections among the Basic Academic Subjects. Teachers may teach in separate departments, but students' thought is probably not divided in the same way.

Finally, the suggestions advanced here generally identify alternate ways of working toward the same outcomes. We wanted very much to avoid any hint that there is one and only one way to achieve the outcomes described in *Academic Preparation for College*. There are many good ways of achieving the desired results, each one good in its own way and in particular circumstances. By describing alternate approaches, we hope to encourage readers of this book to analyze and recombine alternatives and to create the most appropriate and effective approaches, given their own particular situations.

We think that this book and its five companion volumes can be useful to many people. Individual teachers may discover suggestions that will spur their own thought about what might be done in the classroom; small groups of teachers may find the book useful in reconsidering the English program in their high school. It also may provide a takeoff point for in-service sessions. Teachers in several subjects might use it and its companions to explore concerns, such as the Basic Academic Competencies, that range across the high school curriculum. Principals may find these volumes useful in refreshing the knowledge and understanding on which their own instructional leadership is based.

We also hope that these books will prove useful to committees of teachers and officials in local school districts and at the state level who are examining the high school curriculum established in their jurisdictions. Public officials whose decisions directly or indirectly affect the conditions under which teaching and learning occur may find in the books an instructive glimpse of the kinds of things that should be made possible in the classroom.

Colleges and universities may find in all six books occasion to consider not only how they are preparing future teachers, but also whether their own curricula will be suited to students receiving the kinds of preparation these books suggest. But our greatest hope is that this book and its companions will be used as reference points for dialogues between high school and college teachers. It was from such dialogues that *Academic Preparation for College* emerged. We believe that further discussions of this sort can provide a wellspring of insight and energy to move beyond the Green Book toward actually providing the knowledge and skills all students need to be successful in college.

We understand the limitations of the suggestions presented here. Concerning what happens in the classroom, many teachers, researchers, and professional associations can speak with far greater depth and detail than is possible in the pages that follow. This book aspires only to get that conversation going, particularly across the boundaries that usually divide those concerned about education, and especially as it concerns the students who often are least well served. Curriculum, teaching, and learning are far too central to be omitted from the discussion about improving education.

II. Preparation and Outcomes

In recent years, we have arrived at a new view of how young people acquire and use the English language. If learning English was once thought of as a matter of drill and routine, we have come to think of it as remarkable and open, one of life's everyday miracles. Where students were once regarded as blank slates, it is clear now that they arrive in the classroom already immersed in a virtual sea of language and engaged almost unceasingly in the activities that are the special concern of teachers of English. We have come to see, therefore, that the aim of academic preparation in English is less to supply what is not there than to help students discipline and purposefully use their great natural power of language. Although the Green Book lists several outcomes to be sought in the study of English, these are in fact various aspects of a single, large goal. This goal is to help students toward the possession of their own inward standard by which they can chart and control, refine, enjoy, and make effective their use of English.

Like every subject, English makes use of and develops a range of Basic Academic Competencies. The statement on English in the Green Book emphasizes the centrality of reading, writing, and speaking and listening—topics also emphasized in the statement on the Basic Academic Competencies. English, of course, has a chief responsibility for intense work in developing these language skills, but at the same time it seeks its own particular knowledge. This special knowledge includes understanding literature and language itself.

Special knowledge, however, does not mean that literature and language belong to only a few. The predisposition to think of literature as exclusive, or as reserved only for those who feel about it in some preconceived "right" way, is contrary to its enlarging spirit. It also can affect teaching and learning adversely. Unfortunately, research on teaching suggests that favored students often are asked the more challenging questions and are approached with the expectation that they will produce more analytically or aesthetically satisfying responses. This expectation tends to be self-fulfilling and narrows the good that can be done in the classroom. It is important to teach as if all students are capable of intense and rewarding experiences with language and literature, not to continue an old division between some students who are favored and some who are not. All of our students deserve the atmosphere of challenge and response, and literature, when it is well taught, produces exactly this climate.

The arts and skills of English weave among one another, producing a variety of patterns in individual voice and expression. The following discussion distinguishes among them only in order to convey a fuller view of the outcomes described in the Green Book. Separation, however, should not be the point of teaching, nor is it how these outcomes can be best achieved. The interweaving of skills is the key to the curricular approach suggested in Chapter 3 and the pedagogical suggestions made throughout this book. Here we separate one from another only to give a clear sense of the outcomes and for convenience in using the Green Book.

Speaking and Listening

Our students' first experience with language comes in listening and speaking. Moreover, these activities later become the portal through which students enter and engage in the learning of English in the classroom. Therefore, we should be alert to the necessary and inevitable relation between these competencies and the development of skill in reading and writing. Discipline in one influences and helps build skill in the others. Also, we include speaking and listening as a single category to underline the interaction of these two activities on each other.

■ *The ability to engage in discussion as both a speaker and listener—interpreting, analyzing, and summarizing.*

Too much classroom conversation is no more than a competition among monologues; that is, one person waits, perhaps not too patiently, for another to cease speaking so that he or she can begin to talk. We find too little listening, too little speaking in response to what has been previously said. This may be in part because we do not guide our students in genuine discussion. They are rewarded, or believe that they are, for the winning remark, not for how their comments emerge from and add to exchange. In speaking, students need to listen with purpose and to draw on the whole in making their own contributions. The signs of this can be as simple as comments that begin with references such as, "When John said . . ." or, "Elizabeth's earlier remarks make me think that. . . ." Such beginnings are indicative of something very important: the student's ability to tie the thoughts of others together with his or her own. This ability is the start of practice in understanding and interpretation. As discussion carries forward, it brings the student to consideration of how to reach full analysis and synthesis.

- *The ability to contribute to classroom discussions in a way that is readily understood by listeners—that is, succinct and to the point.*

For some students, merely speaking out is enough. It matters little to them that their words contribute nothing to the issue or subject at hand. The reasons vary: a few students are overly fond of their own words, and many others fear the exposure of speaking before peers and teachers. Still, classroom discussion requires that the student and the teacher keep to the point. Without this adherence, there is no developing sense of how language leads to clarity. This warning does not rule out a digression or call for admonishment of everything that is not instantly relevant. Good talk, we know, must sometimes seem to move somewhat away from its center to capture the richness or complexity of an idea. But it is important to ask frequently if what is said improves understanding or keeps it at bay. In this way, students can be helped to develop a sense of pertinence and of its importance in spoken language.

- *The ability to present a position clearly and persuasively.*

Students need to learn to prepare for classroom discussion, much as they prepare for an examination or individual report. Good talk, like good writing, benefits from forethought and the sorting through of one's ideas. When they do speak, students should know that

15

their ideas will receive respectful attention, even though what they say must be subject to question and analysis. Comments, whatever they may be, should not reflect on the speaker personally but rather be addressed to the clarity and completeness of the idea or position presented. In any discussion the responsibility for constructive activity is as much with the listener as with the speaker. As teachers we keep the balance and know that we work with some delicacy to help students speak about their ideas without holding too fast to them or relinquishing them too soon.

- *The ability to recognize the intention of a speaker and to be aware of the techniques a speaker uses to affect an audience.*

Students deserve guidance in recognizing that what they hear is not always reasonable. Speech is a complex action, and students should have experience in evaluating it as actually performed. This can be done through critical attention given to speakers seen on television or in films shown to the class. The evaluation should be as fair as one accorded a classmate; and students should achieve the ability to identify the variety of sources of appeal in oral statements such as voice, demeanor, and delivery. In this way, students should come to appreciate the power of speech and understand that critical care must be taken both with how things are said and how they are heard.

- *The ability to recognize important points and to take good notes in lectures and class discussion.*

We must provide students frequent practice in recognizing important points as they are made both in lecture and class discussion. While students may be familiar with taking lecture notes, many students do not take notes in the less formal exchange of classroom discussion. Understanding an idea or issue partly depends on how well a student follows the thread of remarks from class to class and week to week; but, too often, the words spoken and heard in class are lost to the moment. Taking good notes helps students keep track of the development of ideas and also allows them, at summary moments, to check whether or not they have heard correctly. Moreover, the attention required for putting what one has heard into a few words is itself an aid both to more alert, purposeful listening and to translating aural material into an accurate written statement.

Reading and Literature

■ *The ability to read critically by asking pertinent questions, by recognizing assumptions and implications, and by evaluating ideas.*

A student who has completed high school should have developed critical skill enough to approach a text in the confidence that he or she will learn new things, find fresh insights, and discover something more of the largeness and variety of life. In this, the student should feel that literature is a good companion, a resource, even when it is strange or difficult. Reading, that is, should not be an obstacle to stumble over, but a powerful aid in reaching new understandings and in mastering textual material presented in other areas of study. Achievement in college and later in adult life depends on the ability to apply critical reading skills to a variety of written materials. The ability to read critically should deepen and acquire new shadings throughout one's lifetime. This long, slowly gathering process is fundamental to a developing sense of self and of one's abilities.

The ability to read critically depends on an accurate understanding of the text. Critical reading requires close attention to facts and basic meanings. By the final years of high school, however, recognition and grasp of detail should lead to reasonably insightful reading of texts, not simply the establishment of minimum understanding. Class discussions should go beyond a mere summary of what happens in a story or a statement of the position taken in an essay; they should deal with matters of how meaning is being conveyed. In reading almost any text, for example, it is important to ask questions about voice, tone, and point of view. These considerations, and many others familiar to teachers of English, have a subtle influence on the meaning of a text.

It is sometimes necessary to ask at what level students should deal with ideas and literature. What is to our purpose here is that students, through reading, come to grasp ideas as living things, susceptible to growth and development by their very nature, and showing this nature most by their tendency to change over time and in different hands. For example, many students read Shakespeare's *Macbeth*. They should recognize that it is a work full of ideas and assumptions. One, for example, is that the order and well-being of a state are related to the mental order and balance of its leaders. Students should acquire some understanding of this idea by seeing how it motivates the characters of the play to take particular action. In discussion, we may also ask if the idea has any currency in our own time and circumstance. Do we, for example, often attribute the erratic or violent behavior of a state to the mental or emotional instability of its leader? If so, how does this relate to the idea as it is expressed in *Macbeth?* Does reference from one to the other add to understanding or tend to mislead? These kinds of questions help to make reading a critical and living act.

- *The ability to read a text analytically, recognizing the relationship between form and content.*

By the time they finish high school, students should recognize that reading is more than simple decoding. They must understand that language is various in its means and potent in resources. This involves recognizing how tone affects meaning, the connotation of words, and the difference between literal and figurative meanings. In a somewhat larger sense, it involves having a sense of the relation between form and content. For example, students should see that poetry often relies on a compression of language, and reading it relies on finding out how a few words can express a great deal; that drama does not have a narrator to convey a character's motives; that the novel often looks at its subject from the point of view of a single character to avoid the presumption of omniscience. These things point to values: the concentration on a few words in poetry draws out their many shades of meaning; the devotion to talk in drama reveals how much meaning in language is made *between* people as well as within individuals; the control of point of view in the novel maintains a respect for meaning that is felt as much as it is consciously known.

■ *The knowledge of a range of literature, rich in quality, sensitive to time, and representative of different literary forms and a variety of cultures.*

Recognizing the relation between form and content requires that students experience a number of literary genres—drama, both tragic and comic; poetry; biography and autobiography; and narrative fiction. They also should know something of myth, legend, and folk tales. The works should be not only American and British but also texts from other cultures, both near to us and distant in tradition. They should be modern and ancient, sampling the conventional and absurd in human affairs. High school students cannot be masters of the world's literature, or of any single part of it; but they should know how to recognize its forms and how to take advantage of its variety.

■ *Interest in and sense of curiosity about written work.*

Every English teacher hopes that students will enjoy reading and will take books from the shelves to explore on their own. That we have this image is not entirely a fantasy. We have all seen it; it does happen—perhaps most intensely when a book, in subject and voice, captures a critical moment in the life of a reader. We should not be afraid to admit this intensity into the classroom. Relevance may have been stressed too often in our immediate past, but there *is* importance in the recognition that different times and places have their own books. A curriculum should not be built from particular tastes, but the spark that ignites a student reader can be just this intersection of text and personal experience. It can be the start of independent reading, of avid search, of lifelong return to literature for knowledge and understanding.

■ *The capacity to respond actively and imaginatively to literature.*

What do our students look like when they are interested in reading, when they are responding actively and imaginatively to literature? What are some of the many things we see them doing?

– talking about what they are reading as it affects their thinking, their values, their relationships.

- seeking from their teachers and friends books similar to others that have interested them.
- relating what they are reading to other things they have read.
- comparing what they are reading to what they are experiencing in their own lives.
- testing the sense of what authors are saying against personal experience and beliefs.
- growing in their use of poetic language; making metaphors.
- combining what they are learning in their reading with what they learn from other media: film, television, and music.
- incorporating ideas from their reading into their everyday conversation.

Such students note that what they have read has angered, delighted, saddened, or disturbed them, and they seek an explanation for their reactions—in the author's words, in their own beliefs, in their own hopes. Further, they search for relationships between what they have read and their own lives and the lives of those around them. They imagine the scenes presented, accept the feelings of characters and their motivations, understand that in a world different from their own other attitudes may exist and sometimes prevail. They use their imaginations to become part of the world created for them by the book and make the book, in turn, a part of their own world.

For example, young people reading Heller's *Catch 22* or Kafka's *The Trial* may be informed about their own feelings when they learn that such people, admired writers, have thought of the world as a lunatic asylum or an absurd conspiracy. It is not that they have become convinced that the world is insane but, rather, that they understand that it is part of life to think these thoughts, that other people—great people—have had and continue to have them. Such visions allow them to test what they do and do not believe.

Writing

■ *The recognition that writing is a process involving a number of elements, including collecting information and formulating ideas, determining their relationships, drafting, arranging paragraphs in an appropriate order and building transitions between them, and revising what has been written.*

Students should recognize that writing is not something that happens merely by taking up pen and paper. Writing requires preparation and planning before one begins to put words together and revision and editing after one has put the words on paper. In other words, writing is not a single, instantaneous act; it is a sequence of stages, a process.

Before the actual writing begins, writers must gather information and impressions; must sort through this material, whatever its kind; must decide the what and how of approaching it; must do all that will enable them to decide what the finished piece should be like. For each individual, this part of the process will be different. Some work from full note cards; others think things through on long, solitary walks. Many write in an unstructured way to find out what they want to say. Usually preparation involves a combination of several things. By the end of high school, students need to have a good sense both of the need for planning and what approach works best for them.

Students also need to appreciate that moving from the planning stage to a final edited product frequently involves making many drafts of the same paper. This, they need to recognize, is not mere mechanical drudgery but a necessary part of discovering what they have to say. Drafting relieves them of the mistaken belief that things should come on the first try and permits them the advantages of trial and error. Central to the idea of drafting is the ability not only to produce an idea but also to do it justice through gradual elaboration of its elements and implications.

Finally, students need to practice and understand the difference between rewriting and editing. This can be difficult. Sometimes a draft needs only minor editorial changes; other times it may require radical revision. It takes some toughness to subject one's work to this kind of scrutiny. Moreover, after much effort, it is not easy to keep a clear, fresh eye. Still, students need to develop approaches and standards through which they can carry out effective self-appraisal. As part of this development, they should incorporate reference to outside resources such as handbooks, peer readers, etc. In the final result, however, self-appraisal rests with one's own observation and reflection.

- *The recognition of writing as a way of discovering and clarifying ideas.*

Most of us have had the experience of understanding what we thought we knew only after we had written it out. Writing can be discovery, a way of revealing one's ideas even to oneself. We do not fully understand this close alliance of thought and writing, but experience tells us that it exists. This is one of the reasons we think of writing as a natural power. It is also why we place such importance on drafting. This permits not only corrections and amendments but also a deepening of thought and gradual elaboration of ideas.

- *The ability to write appropriately for different occasions, audiences, and purposes.*

We need to provide our students ample and repeated practice in various kinds of writing. We must ask them to use language for different purposes: to describe, to persuade, to narrate, to explain a position or idea. This should acquaint them with the different requirements of different writing tasks and give them practice in adding versatility to their basic writing abilities. A single approach to writing will not adequately meet the many writing demands that will be made on them in life.

One good way to approach this matter is for the writer to become aware of the audience. In describing a place, for example, would students do it in the same way for a close friend, a parent, a stranger? In actually doing such writing, they become aware of the need to use a different tone and present different information. They need also to develop a sense of occasion. Is the writing done in a moment of celebration, of need, of obligation? This, too, will affect how it should be done and what approach the student takes to the writing.

- *Skill and assurance in using the conventions of standard written English.*

Students need to acquire knowledge of the conventions of written communications and understand how these conventions bring reasonable order to written language. This knowledge involves mastery of such matters as punctuation, spelling, agreement of subject and verb, and control of tense. We know that students are achieving skill and assurance in the conventions of standard written English when they use them naturally and smoothly in their papers, when they raise questions about flexibility in the use of a convention, and when they demonstrate recognition that the use of conventions is conditioned by purpose.

Language

- *English, like every other language, operates according to grammatical systems and patterns of usage.*

Students need to learn that the English language has grammatical systems and that they should understand these systems and apply them every day. They should acquire a vocabulary for describing these systems, using such terms as *verb, preposition, linking verb, stress,* and *inflection.* They need also to be aware of such matters as the following:

– how an English verb signals tense.
– how an English speaker signals that a question is being asked.
– how words are most frequently ordered in an English sentence.

Students need to learn both that spoken English differs from written English and that the difference can be identified. Students need to know what slang is, what jargon is, what regionalisms are, what standard English is, and what occasions will make the use of any one of them appropriate or inappropriate.

- *English continues to undergo change.*

We need to devise activities that enable students to realize that no living language is static and that English is no exception. They should know the following.

– New words are added to the language every day from various sources.
– What was once unacceptable English may be acceptable today.

- What was once acceptable English may be unacceptable today.
- Words change in meaning or even go out of use.
- Conventions of the written language change.
- Patterns of usage change.

■ *English is influenced by other languages, both ancient and modern.*

The more students are encouraged to read and discuss language, the more they will discover that commerce among peoples tends to cause changes in language. For example, English owes many of its words to French, which was the language of the Norman conquerors of England. American English owes words such as *ranch, rodeo,* and *mesa* to the Spanish-speaking settlers of the Southwest. Students should also be aware of the significance of root words, prefixes, and suffixes that come from Greek and Latin, and that these inheritances have given names to things those ancient peoples had never heard of: television, xerography, astronaut, and automatic transmission, for example.

■ *English has several levels of usage, and consequently the language appropriate in some situations may not be appropriate in others.*

With sufficient practice, students should come to know the occasions and audiences appropriate for using different levels of language. For example, highly informal language is inappropriate in business correspondence, which may be between friends, but which also serves as an official record. Highly formal language is inappropriate in conversations among family members. Students should learn that the level of usage employed must take into account both the relationship between the parties sharing the communication and the nature and purpose of the communication.

■ *English has many dialects.*

The dialects of English are, like the dialects of other languages, variations that have their own grammars and their own vocabularies. We must help our students to see that nearly all spoken language is dialect and that there are indeed many dialects in America. Students should practice recognizing dialects, become conscious of their own dialects, and grow in understanding the appropriate use or avoidance of dialect in different contexts.

Specifically, students should be aware of the following.

- The language that is now considered standard English is of historical origin.
- The dialect considered standard has a usefulness in that it permits ease of communication among English speakers.
- Other dialects are different from the standard dialect but are not necessarily better or worse.
- Some dialects are used to preserve cultural or regional identity.
- Dialects have a social history as well as a linguistic one.

■ *English words, like those of other languages, gather meaning from their context and carry connotation.*

Like everyone else, students increase their vocabularies by hearing others speak the language and reading what others have written. They learn what words mean, not by memorizing a list but by hearing or reading words in context. They learn that, though words may be close in definition, they often convey very different meanings, that there is a significant difference between *slender* and *skinny* and between *observing* and *watching*. In the same way, students learn to distinguish between being nervous and being nerved, and between pursuing a goal and pursuing a criminal. Moreover, students should become aware that, given the context of other statements and considering the tone, a word can be so transformed in meaning that it suggests the very opposite of its literal meaning.

A Final Note

The arts and skills described in this section are not acquired in the short space of four years in high school. Students whom teachers meet in grade nine need to have made great progress in acquiring these very competencies long before they left the eighth grade. What students do on reaching high school differs in degree and complexity, but it is consistent in kind. For this reason, it is important that teachers at all levels of our schools come to agreement about the competencies students need and act in concert in helping students to achieve them.

III. The Curriculum

In considering desired learning outcomes, we inevitably begin to ask questions about the high school curriculum in English. Our purpose in this chapter is not to prescribe answers to these questions, but to encourage and inform discussion. Sometimes, of course, it almost seems that discussion about the English curriculum might go on without us. We hear much these days from many quarters about what should be happening in our classrooms. This should not surprise us, for, in a most important sense, this is testimony to the vital nature of the work we do. What is essential is that we remain at the center of action regarding curriculum. We have always been mindful of our teaching, and now is not the time to step back from questions about the organization of study in English.

We are not in present danger of doing so. As Arthur Applebee suggested in his history of the teaching of English,[1] the influence of the subject on those who teach it is "too consuming" to think that curriculum discussions among faculty will ever be anything but intense and wide-ranging. The major problem we face is not one of will or interest, but of time. School time is heavily scheduled, and much of after-school time must be devoted to unit planning and reading student papers. This means that we lack adequate opportunity to join with our colleagues in the careful, but often tough, sorting out of curriculum issues that most of us want. Curriculum, as we know, cannot be made by a single teacher, scholar, or administrator. It is by definition a collegial and collaborative enterprise.

Even to say that our curriculum is made collaboratively may not do justice to actual conditions. In his study of schools in action,

---

1. Arthur N. Applebee, *Tradition and Reform in the Teaching of English: A History* (Urbana, Illinois: National Council of Teachers of English, 1974), p. 255.

John Goodlad observed that there are actually five different curricula occurring simultaneously in any school setting.[2]

1. The Ideal Curriculum (what scholars believe should be taught).
2. The Formal Curriculum (what some monitoring agency, such as the state or local district, has prescribed).
3. The Perceived Curriculum (what teachers believe they are teaching in response to student needs).
4. The Operational Curriculum (what an outside observer sees being taught in the classroom).
5. The Experiential Curriculum (what the students believe they are learning).

These different curricula, of course, do not go forward in splendid isolation from one another. Indeed, they are all part of the general buzz, and it would not be unusual to hear a single teacher speak from the point of view of all five during the course of a single curriculum meeting. This does not suggest confusion, but rather that we implicitly recognize the many contributors to the discussion about what is to be studied and how it is to be organized.

Still, it stands to reason that the classroom teacher is in the best position to combine the five points of view and give them effective meaning in curriculum development. This does not suggest that teachers must assemble and analyze all that could be written under the five headings in making decisions. It may be useful, however, for teachers to refer to the following grid when they meet to address curriculum.

Ideal
Findings from current research in the teaching of English.

Formal
State and local mandates concerning skills in English.

Perceived
List of greatest strengths and weaknesses of students; list of most successful and least successful of our teaching attempts.

---

2. John Goodlad, *A Place Called School* (New York: McGraw-Hill, 1984).

| *Operational* | What others have noted in evaluation reports, such as accrediting agency reports and reports from local supervisors. |
| *Experiential* | What students say in formal or informal course evaluation. |

We do not have to agree entirely with the labels or definitions to know that such a grid can help us locate comments and arrange priorities within a more complete view. It may also alert us to a consideration we have forgotten or a bit of research we need to do. Finally, we may discover ways that the grid helps to conserve time— whether by suggesting a focus, framing the subject, or charting the ground to be covered.

We customarily think of curriculum as an assembly of courses. In this country, these courses have never been rigidly fixed in content. They have been open particularly to changes in scholarly and intellectual interests. For instance, various currents of thought have influenced the what and how of reading in our recent history— sociology in the thirties, semantics in the forties, new criticism in the fifties and sixties, and eclecticism in the seventies that resulted in a proliferation of elective courses including such things as science fiction and the literature of rock music. To some, this repeated "reform" of curriculum indicates a lack of coherence and a low regard for tradition; to others it reflects a healthy willingness to reconsider and act on the changing needs of a vital and diverse culture. This debate will very probably continue far into the future. Even so, we believe that it is possible to organize the English curriculum with reference to understood aims and outcomes and that the many constituencies interested in curriculum making can be brought to share in these understandings.

Aims

The English curriculum should be enabling. It is important not just that students are presented with information but that they are able to use information to read and write effectively, reason clearly, and think reflectively; it is important not just that students possess a certain arrangement of academic credits but that they become independent learners. In this spirit, we suggest that the aim of the secondary curriculum should be to enable students to do the following.

- Acquire poise and confidence in the various language activities.
- Recognize and make use of the interrelatedness of competence in reading, writing, speaking, listening, reasoning, studying, and observing.
- Recognize and make use of the relation of skills learned in the English class to the practice of these same skills in other academic subjects and in their lives outside school.
- Develop sound standards of appraisal, both for their own use of language and for the use of language by others.
- Discover through language and literature a better understanding of themselves, of others, and of the worlds they enter and inhabit.

General Curriculum Considerations

Though we do not attempt to define the curriculum—for that is the task of teachers working within the context of their departments and localities—we wish to present several general considerations bearing on what is taught and how it is organized. We begin, of course, with the description of the subject of English in Chapter 2. With this as the context, perhaps most of us can give general assent to James Moffett's idea that the language arts involve two receptive and two productive activities; reading and listening for receiving the language of others; speaking and writing for verbalizing and expressing our own thoughts and feelings. In addition, we also probably agree with Moffett that thinking informs all four of these activities, serving in essential ways as their common denominator.[3] Our challenge is to consider what content effectively serves the development of the receptive and productive activities, how to

---

3. James Moffett and Betty Jane Wagner, *Student-Centered Language Arts and Reading, K-13: A Handbook for Teachers*, 2nd ed. (Boston: Houghton Mifflin, 1976), p. 13.

arrange it over a period of three or four years, and to what degree we should emphasize one activity or teaching approach over another.

This challenge includes several obvious but important questions. Should the productive or receptive modes of language predominate in the curriculum? Should one precede the other? Within each, is one activity—say, reading—more important than listening? How do we know which to use as a point of departure in designing a program in English for the college-bound?

Because the language arts are interrelated, it is difficult, and probably unwise, to argue that one is more important than another or that one should precede the other in helping students to achieve greater ability in thought and expression. As Moffett points out, "Practice of the activities of speaking, writing, listening, performing, and reading is not only the means to the goal but also the goal itself. All five processes are goals, and yet each can be a means to the others. People can learn to write by talking, to read by listening, to spell by reading, and so on."[4] (Examples of specific teaching exercises that build from this interrelatedness are included in Chapters 4 and 5.)

Given this orientation, it will be necessary to modify our notion of curriculum as a linear experience, with a structure of skills marking stages of hierarchical development. In addition, we must pay increasing attention to the *balance* between reading and writing within the English curriculum, and their *integration* with speaking and listening, if we are to come closer to achieving the desired outcomes. Reading and writing may be emphasized (as discussed below), but not in disregard of listening and speaking. Instead, since each activity may include, and rely on, one or more of the others, the organizing principles of a curriculum should emphasize the interaction between and among receptive and productive processes.

Particularly, we need to conceive of language study as a *recursive* process—that is, as development that occurs through learning activities at all grade levels, which differ less in kind than in

---

4. Moffett and Wagner, p. 48.

degree and complexity. This asks us to think of language as having fullness, which we experience through a process of repeated return, instead of as a structure that we scale through a sequence of definite steps. For example, we might ask a tenth grader, a twelfth grader, and a college sophomore the same question about a poem: Who is speaking? And we might be satisfied if the tenth grader told us that the speaker in Richard Wilbur's "Boy at the Window" is a young boy. We would be less than satisfied if the twelfth grader told us only that the speaker in Richard Eberhart's "The Groundhog" was an adult male, and still less so if the sophomore told us the person in Frost's "Stopping by Woods on a Snowy Evening" was simply Frost himself. Given the same kinds of questions over a period of years, with the concerted attention of teachers, a student should provide increasingly full and layered responses.

We might approach in the same way the assignment in Chapter 5 in which students are asked to write about a place central to their life and culture. For a tenth grader, we might be happy with a clear statement and good organization. With the high school senior, who has had more practice, we would expect something of greater detail, virtuosity, and reflectiveness. The point is that students in all grade levels can and should be asked to do similar things with language. Not the task, but the result or outcome changes. In this way, we do not think of the curriculum in terms of adding discrete components of skill one after another, but rather as an unfolding in which we attempt, as Applebee puts it, to "gradually elaborate the linguistic and intellectual repertoire of our students, a process that is more fluid than linear, more fortuitous than predictable."[5]

It follows, then, that curriculum is not only an assembly of courses, but also *a set of recurring questions and tasks.* Teachers of English should be given and make use of the time to frame these questions and to form pedagogical approaches to them. This care should bring curriculum into closer correspondence with the reality of language development, particularly with the way language abilities deepen through time. In addition, it should permit students to compile portfolios of work that could be reviewed at intervals over

---

5. Applebee, p. 254.

a relatively long period of time. If students can look at their performance on similar tasks at one- or two-year intervals, they can begin to get a better grasp of what "development" means and also move forward in acquiring standards of self-appraisal. Finally, the recurrence of critical questions and assignments might do something to relieve "either you get it or you don't" problems. No student, or any of us, ever gets it all; and for students who have gotten lost, a recursive approval provides a chance to recover some ground or at least to know that school can repeat its opportunities.

Speaking and Listening: Further Considerations

Of the academic competencies, it is very probable that reading and writing will continue to predominate in the explicit curriculum. These competencies have been our traditional emphases, and both colleges and the public hold us more accountable for them than for anything else. What then do we do about speaking and listening, if we are to gain some better balance among skills overall in our teaching activities? The answer, for the moment, is probably that we include them implicitly whenever possible in the student's experience of reading and writing. Though the listing is somewhat schematic, consider for instance the various functions of oral discourse listed by Glatthorn:[6] heuristic (finding things out), personal (expressing personality), informational (conveying information), interactional (maintaining relationships), and regulatory (controlling others' behavior). Regardless of whether or not this is a complete list, it does suggest the complexity of speech and the many ways we use it. At certain times we may develop lessons that focus on one or more of these functions, but, more to the point, we can return from time to time in all our class discussions to remark on how things are being said and heeded. This in itself should gradually

---

6. Allan A. Glatthorn, *A Guide for Developing an English Curriculum for the Eighties* (Urbana, Illinois: National Council of Teachers of English, 1980).

increase student recognition of the richness of spoken language and
the possibility of increased achievement in its use.[7]

Reading: Further Considerations

Much of our thinking about reading in the curriculum focuses on
what books and texts should be used in its teaching. On this matter,
we want to comment on two issues: textbooks and a core curriculum.

Use of Anthologies

We have long been concerned about the extent to which the curriculum in reading is textbook-driven. Unfortunately, books are
expensive, and as a result the use of anthologies prevails in most
school systems. These anthologies typically present literature in
one of a small number of formats: according to literary genre,
literary theme, or literary history. Such "formatting" also influences
readings in school systems that can afford the use of individual
paperback texts. While there is nothing necessarily wrong with
these ways of ordering literature, no single one of them should
predetermine questions of what and how books are read. Students
need experience with all these approaches. Teachers should regularly review the curriculum to make certain that textbooks offered
by publishers will not have the first and last word about what can
be done. Where using an anthology is almost the sole recourse,
school administrators must give English teachers time to develop
approaches to its use that achieve the aims of the school and its

---

7. We may also explore associations in the ways language is read, written, spoken,
and heard. Again, consider Glatthorn's listing of kinds of listening: appreciative,
discriminative, comprehensive, therapeutic, and critical (p. 13). These same functions could be used to illuminate current theories concerning both reader response
and approaches to writing. Specific examples of how attention to speaking and
listening can be incorporated in actual teaching situations are included in Chapters
4 and 5.

curriculum. Given inventive adaptation of what is available, students should not read only excerpts from complete literary texts or selections ordered and understood entirely through a single format.

Core Curriculum

There is, as we know, a good deal of debate currently about whether curriculum in general should be organized around a "common core" of learning and whether the English curriculum, for its part, should adopt a list of authors defined as classic or "great." We do not find it easy to say whether the academic outcomes set forth in the Green Book are compatible with this approach or, in some important ways, stand in disagreement with it. Certainly, those who argue for a "common core" have a legitimate, even urgent, concern: how can students address critical questions, make comparisons, and draw contrasts if they do not have a knowledge base or a context of learning that is shared with other students and teachers? This question needs to be searched through as we think about what is to be read. Several questions, however, have to be addressed at the same time.

- Is a "national" reading list consistent with, or reflective of, a culture as diverse as our own? How could such a list represent our variety of regions, heritage, and social situations? Perhaps most to the point, how could it reflect the varieties of literature and voices that have emerged from this variety of conditions—that is, how could it reflect literature itself?

- Is it more important in a culture such as ours that literature assists readers to find and hold common ground or that it helps them to understand and respect the fact that others may live, think, and react differently from themselves? The answer surely is that both outcomes are equally important. But which is more likely to achieve a balance: a national reading list or one developed at the local level?

- There is a tendency on the part of advocates of a national list to emphasize classic readings, texts from the past, books that have proved their worth by lasting. The books cited are unquestionably worthy and have our allegiance, but how does this heavy preponderance of works from the past demonstrate that literature is living, vital, and changing in its relations to contemporary life and issues? One does not have to think classic texts irrelevant to current situations in order to believe that student readers also need the experience of literature in its continuing attempt to understand our times.

■ Finally, there is the matter of heritage itself. In drawing heavily from the past, a national reading list might look largely to our Anglo-American traditions. This background is essential, but any look at current demographics suggests strongly that it is only a part of our literary heritage. What about African, Hispanic, and Asian strands? What about the full reach of European heritage, the effect on us of cultural centers such as Vienna, Prague, and so on? Must we not offer students Kafka and Freud as well as Hawthorne and Jane Austen? It may be too vague to say that our perspective must be global, but do we not have to make an attempt to include all that we have become?

Generic Questions about Reading

We have suggested that the teaching of English can be organized with reference to a set of recurring questions. The following is a list of such questions. While they do not in themselves constitute a curriculum, they suggest points of emphasis that a curriculum might contain. As noted, we do not present them in any prescriptive sense, but rather as a possible means for starting discussion about the structure and substance of curriculum among teachers in local settings.

■ *Who is the speaker? What are some of his or her characteristics?* We ask students to probe, to be analytic in their responses, to explain how they define the characteristics they identify, to state specific reasons and evidence for what they say, to consider how details that the speaker selects help to establish an individual voice.

■ *Who is the audience?* This is often a difficult question, particularly if we will not be satisfied with, "We are; the reader is." For instance, what kind of audience do students imagine the persona of *The Scarlet Letter* has in mind: the narrator of *The Sun Also Rises*, or the speaker in one of Robert Frost's poems, or the narrator of *Native Son?*

- *How does the speaker/narrator feel about other characters and about events?* This, too, is difficult but asks students to draw particulars from narrative and to interpret them: How does Holden Caulfield in *Catcher in the Rye* feel toward adults, schooling, and himself? How does John feel about his society in Benét's "By the Waters of Babylon"?

- *What is the context for the story being told?* There is often no definitive answer to this question, but speculation offers new ways to approach what is being said. For example, what might prompt the narrator of *The Secret Sharer* to tell his story? Why does the narrator of *The Color Purple* tell her story? What does "The Rime of the Ancient Mariner" tell us about the impetus to tell a story?

- *Do you think the writer expected readers to take any action after having read this?* Such a question can lead to discussions of overall structure, of tone, of rhetorical appeal, of reader response, as well as to exposition of what is being communicated by a writer and various ways the readers in this group are interpreting it and responding to it.

Writing: Further Considerations

We hear a good deal these days about the need for students to do a lot of writing in school. All things considered, this is a good thing; but, if approached simplistically, it could reduce curricular considerations merely to questions of quantity—to such things, that is, as how many themes are written in a term or how many class hours are devoted to agreement of subject and verb. These measurements do not produce a context that locates students in the actual process of language acquisition and production. We cannot "manage" students into better writing through scheduled attention to its mechanical elements. Rather, we want to keep them alert and in touch with the motive forces that inform written expression and engender its many uses.

With this intention, we suggest that student writing must "take its time." It must be understood as something that happens through a process or flow of activities, not as a static or prestanding structure that one attempts to reproduce on the page. This view of writing includes the following points.

- Writing is a process that involves analyzing the writing task and the intended audience, focusing an idea, examining what one knows and needs to know about the topic, gathering necessary information, organizing and drafting thought, shaping and reshaping the draft, and editing the final product with regard to purpose, subject, audience, and the relation to standard written English. We organize this flow of activity into the stages of prewriting, writing, and postwriting.[8]

- Over extended periods of teaching time, this process incorporates other activities including observing, talking, listening, note taking, and practice in information gathering. In addition, we guide student practice in other kinds of writing—for example, journal keeping, free and impromptu writing, personal communication. These exercises not only give additional practice in writing but also contribute to recognition of writing as a way of knowing and learning and as a source of personal enjoyment.

- Mere frequency of writing alone helps little to increase student ability. Therefore, we attempt to make the writing process recursive—that is, throughout the curriculum we have students return several times to similar tasks. This method takes into account how ability deepens gradually over time and provides a realistic background for the appraisal of performance and assessment of development. Curriculum development, therefore, centrally involves faculty determination of those writing tasks that are important and worthy to repeat over the three or four years of high school.

---

8. Michael C. Flanigan, "Composition Models: Dynamic and Static Imitations," in *Theory into Practice*, XIX, 3 (Summer 1980), p. 3.

These considerations again raise questions about how we use textbooks in teaching English. The textbooks now available typically approach writing in relation to earlier notions about the teaching of rhetoric. In doing so, they give us much on grammar and mechanics but very little on the process of composition. They tend to draw us toward an emphasis on what makes a correct product rather than to what supports the student through the activity of writing itself. Our curriculum decisions begin to redress this imbalance if they establish the tasks that faculty will undertake with students recurringly during the high school years. We may conclude, for example, that our students should be producing some discursive and some imaginative writing at every grade level; that at every grade level they should explore and experiment with different writing voices; that at times they should have to deal with boundaries of purpose, audience, and occasion that are established by the teacher; and that at other times they should have to determine these boundaries themselves. And we might conclude that, in the total time we have for teaching, our students should have a variety of experiences, ranging from free writing to making an accurate report of what someone has said.

As we become clear about these writing tasks, we are likely to incorporate activities that include the related competencies of speaking, listening, reading, observing—and so to undertake with students a variety of experiences that offer practice in the interrelatedness of the receptive and productive features of language. In doing this, we almost certainly will explore different kinds of appraisal and evaluation. We might ask students to assume different roles as they work with what they and others have written—now as critic, now as proofreader, now as editor. This, in turn, varies our own part in the teaching process: sometimes we act as stimulus, at other times as consultant, at still other times as arbiter. That is, we serve as teacher—not simply as the marker of papers.

Generic Questions to Ask about Writing

As in the case of reading, there are generic questions about writing that can inform our discussions about curriculum. We attach special importance to the following.

- *Invention and prewriting. How does a writer think of what to say?* A writer reviews materials at hand, collects or is reminded of more material while writing goes on. Thinking back over experience, reading further, talking with others—all these are ways to help invention occur.

- *Focusing on a subject. What does a writer emphasize?* Focus involves questions about purpose, aim, intent. The same material is open to development in many different ways. What is one's thesis or attitude toward the subject? For example, the travel narrative in Chapter 4 is about human relationships, but with a different purpose in mind it could focus on places, things, or cultural differences.

- *Organization and development. How does a writer decide on sequence and put words together?* A writer divides what there is to say into parts, tries to see how those parts fit together logically or follow from each other, tries to think as a reader would and to see what part of a subject needs to be known before another part can be understood. The process involves true organization, not merely "beginning, middle, and end" or "five-paragraph theme."

- *Revision. What does this have to do with being a writer?* A writer revises because there is more to say—he has realized something; she has thought of a better way to put it. Revision occurs at any of several stages: as material is being gathered and its organization mapped out, as strategies of presentation emerge, or as a reader's needs are thought about. There may be many drafts, complete or incomplete, with or without the reactions of an intended audience. All this revision is substantial, and thus different from merely editing, which is also needed to control the formal and mechanical aspects of language.

- *How does a writer know what to do?* We can help by dividing a complex process into identifiable parts, even though we keep assuring our students that it all happens at once. We can focus at different times on the aims of a writer or the purposes of writing and the ways they change from subject to subject; on the audience or reader a writer is thinking of (and by this means help our students realize that they do write to be read and therefore must deal with rhetoric and the negotiations between argument and persuasion); on the modes a writer may use (narration, exposition, or description); on the means available (illustration, evidence, or figurative language).

A Final Note

In conclusion we return to where we began. We must deal with issues of curriculum ourselves. In an ideal world, teachers from all grade levels would meet in their own schools to discuss the balance, integration, and recursiveness of language experiences in their curriculum. They would speculate on grade-level outcomes and grade-entry expectations. They would peruse student portfolios containing evidence of student effort and achievement and papers from various years. They would analyze content to see that needless repetition does not occur across the English curriculum, but that the reading, writing, speaking, and listening activities that bear repeating are, in fact, repeated from year to year. And they would share both their more promising practices and their most disappointing attempts in teaching the curriculum.

We are still some distance from the ideal, of course, but we have come a long way. As Applebee reminds us,

> . . . in its brief history as a school subject, English has responded openly to changing pedagogical and social concerns, assimilating and redefining them as necessary. Though its very openness has led to many false starts and temporary diversions—even a propensity for fads and gimmicks—over the long term it has shed the distortions of one point of view after another. . . . Today's teachers of English are better trained than their predecessors, with a stronger national organization and a more professionally oriented body of colleagues than at any previous time. Though the shape of the new English may be unclear from the perspective of the present, the next chapters of this history, when they are written, will surely describe a curriculum better than any we have seen in the past.[9]

---

9. Applebee, p. 255.

IV. Teaching English

In this chapter we present teaching plans for learning in reading and writing—two plans for reading and two for writing. In each case the two plans complement one another, and the one builds on achievement in the other. These plans integrate development of speaking and listening skills, and teachers can extend them by fashioning opportunities to call attention explicitly to the language outcomes discussed in Chapter 2 (pages 23-25). It may seem to our readers that what we describe is more than a "plan"—that, indeed, it contains some projection or imagining of what might happen as these assignments are carried forward in a classroom setting. This is correct: we hope to escape the abstractness that characterizes many class-planning documents.

These plans do not presume to represent *the* ideal teaching approach or situation. Obviously, we believe that they are effective teaching strategies; but we do not think of them as either the "best" or the only possibilities for going about our work. Effective teaching takes place in a variety of ways. It may be achieved in teacher-centered lecture, shared between teacher and class in a discussion, or emerge among small groups working on specific tasks. The list could grow very long. Our purpose is not to name the many strategies or to single out one over another, but to be specific enough to deepen discussion about how curriculum can be translated into the particularities of class planning.

Writing

The plans presented here rest on assumptions explained in Chapters 2 and 3. In teaching the arts and skills of English we draw on their natural interrelation. Because the connections are already there, they are best taught for what they are: interrelated functions of the complicated invention that is language. For instance, a teacher might use an overhead projector or multigraphed copies in order to give students the chance to analyze one another's papers. Discussion about those papers provides practice in close reading, as students look at each other's papers to analyze what is said in them and how it is said. The same discussion provides practice in listening and speaking. Most of this practice (as practice) goes unnoticed, for attention is on writing strategies. But the option is open to call attention to ways that these activities themselves are complicated uses of language in its various modes. There are times when we should call this to students' attention. In this way we use ordinary classroom moments to build on and emphasize the inter-relation of skills.

The analytic questions used in discussion of a student's paper are themselves tools.

- They require generalization based on information. What is this paragraph about?
- They require detail used as supporting evidence. How is that subject referred to in this paragraph? Does everything in the paragraph refer to that subject only?
- They result in judgments. Is the subject developed so that you understand it? Are there ways it could be more completely or effectively developed?

Such questions ask for responses ranging from informational to evaluative. At times, we may need to make the intention of the question explicit in order to bring attention to the skill involved.

Discussion of writing relies on samples, including students' own papers. It arises from informal and formal occasions: impromptu papers, assigned papers, journals written from day to day either in free response or in answer to questions. Discussion of specific papers recognizes that writing is a process and calls attention to as many stages of that process as possible. At the same time, discussion of papers emphasizes that language skills are interrelated: writing is under focus, but partly by means of speaking and listening resulting from reading.

The plans that follow are based on the generic questions about writing listed in Chapter 3. Readers may want to refer to these questions as they consider this material.

Plan I: Prewriting and Problem Solving

In this plan, we devote a full class session to discussing practical problem solving with the students. The teacher begins by describing a problem that he or she has recently solved—some common, easily understood problem such as finding a way around heavy traffic on the way to school in the morning or living with five other people in an apartment intended for three. The teacher then asks for problems that members of the class or people they know have solved. In discussion, attention should focus on getting the problem stated clearly and reconstructing the sequence of events involved in attempting solutions. The teacher helps students clarify the various things they did as part of their resolutions of problems: thinking about the situation, trying alternatives, searching for information, consulting with others, experimenting, leaving and coming back to the problem. The point of such discussion is to help students prewrite for a paper in which they will describe a problem they have solved. After talking about problem solving in this way, the teacher gives the following assignment to the students.

Directions: Consider a problem that you often face and that you have solved. Write a paper, probably two to three pages long, in which you do the following:

1. State the problem clearly.
2. Describe what you had to find out in order to solve the problem.
3. Describe any early attempts at solution that were not solutions and what you found out from them.
4. Describe how you modified what you were doing and did find a solution.

As you write your paper, remember our class discussion of solving a problem and write so that your classmates can follow what you are describing and explaining.

When the students turn in their papers, the teacher discusses ways that writing the paper itself involved solving a problem. The assignment included a number of stages to be described. Did students find that in writing about each of them, they went through a series of stages not so different from the ones they were describing? Such discussion asks students to think about problem solving as a process, as something they were doing as they described doing it. It also asks them to think about abstractions and about the ways that various specifics are instances of the same abstractions.

An assignment like this introduces the idea of problem solving and asks for instances of it. It shows by the form of the assignment that what is to be presented has different parts, and it provides a built-in structure as practice in orderly presentation. It also makes special use of prewriting—working through in class the stages each student will go through later in writing a longer paper.

A suggestion: write out the assignment. Then all students can be sure of what they are expected to do, and their papers can be read from a common perspective.

Plan II: A Group Narrative: Improving the Development of Ideas

Students often have little trouble in reading narrative writing but produce a loosely strung sequence of events when asked to explain something by means of narrative. These accounts offer a reader little more than a time-log of an action. Written exercises combining both individual and group activity vary the usual assignment and demonstrate ways to develop a time-log into a narrative.

Terror on Wheels

In the exercise below, the students are divided into five separate groups, and each group is invited to rewrite a portion of a narrative.

Step 1. Distribute the following narrative to the students, and discuss the reasons why it is uninteresting and ineffectual, even though it has the basic features of narrative writing and contains no mechanical errors.

> Our most recent family vacation was one I shall never forget. We left our peaceful home in Chicago and headed south, our destination being Disney World in Florida. The trip in the car was pleasant enough, except for the constant annoyances of my little brother, who is just too young to be confined in the back seat of a car for more than an hour at a time.
>
> The real joy of the trip was Disney World itself. There was literally something for everybody in the family—games and rides for my brother,

exhibitions for my father, shopping for my mother and me, and wonderful food for everyone. We spent a total of three days there, leisurely taking in the sights and eating ourselves into obesity.

When the time came to start our return trip, I think none of us was quite ready to leave the fantasy atmosphere we had quickly adjusted to at Disney World, but Dad always says, "There's no such thing as a free lunch," and I guess he's right. In less than a week from the time we left Disney World, I would be entering my senior year, my brother would be back at school, and Mom and Dad would be back at work. I know we all hope to return to Disney World at the first opportunity.

Step 2. Ask the students to count off by fives. Then explain that each of the five groups is going to be given part of a rewritten version of the family trip story that they have just read. However, each group will receive only the *beginning* and *ending* of their segment of the narrative. Their task will be to write material connecting the beginning and the ending of their portion of the story. This exercise is designed to help students think imaginatively about narrative development and to write in more interesting and effective ways.

Step 3. Read the following introduction to the narrative aloud to the class.

The world's greatest individuals—from Joan of Arc to Winston Churchill to Martin Luther King—for all the heroism they have shown under extreme pressure, have nothing on me. I call myself a super-hero, because I have lived to write about my experience supervising an eight-year-old brother on a 2,000 mile journey with our mother and father in a 1974, two-door Dodge Duster. That I lived through it is remarkable; that I can write about it is miraculous.

Step 4. Distribute to Group I their portion of the narrative material provided below; distribute to Group II the second portion of the narrative, and so on. Then ask the students to each write *their own version* of the portion of the story for which they have been given the beginning and ending.

Step 5. Ask the students in each group to read their version of the story to the other members of the group. The group must then select one of these versions to read to the class. Give the groups about ten minutes to complete this process.

Step 6. Have the representative from each group read the beginning of the segment that the group received, the connective material that was written by one of the members of the group, and the concluding portion of the segment that they were given. The story will then unfold as follows, with Group V supplying the conclusion to the story.

Group I reader:

(Beginning of segment 1): "My troubles began when I discovered that my first responsibility was getting my brother ready for the trip."

(Next comes the connecting material written by a member of the group.)

(End of segment 1): "Finally, I took a deep breath and repeated to myself: 'It's only for a week, it's only for a week, it's only for a week.' "

Group II reader:

(Beginning of segment 2): "If you think it was bad getting an eight-year-old ready for a long trip like this, just consider what I had to face when we finally got into the car."

(Next comes the connecting material written by a member of the group.)

(End of segment 2): "After this, no one should be surprised that by nighttime, when we reached the motel in Knoxville, I felt as if I had taken one giant step toward insanity."

Group III reader:

(Beginning of segment 3): "But I had a lot to learn about insanity. The minute we crawled out of the car, my dad cheered me up with the news that my brother and I were sharing a room."

(Next comes the connecting material written by a member of the group.)

(End of segment 3): "Dawn's early light came none too early."

Group IV reader:

(Beginning of segment 4): "Writing off the first half of the trip as a real nightmare, I promised myself that I would take a different approach for the rest of our journey—I resolved to think positively and notice only the good things about my little brother. It didn't work: my efforts led straight to disaster."

(Next comes the connecting material written by a member of the group.)

(End of segment 4): "By the time we reached Disney World, my thoughts were in turmoil. What should I do?"

Group V reader:

(Beginning of segment 5): "I thought carefully about all that I had learned through this harrowing experience and set up a few general policies, which I knew I could safely follow during the trip home. I hope that they are useful to anyone who is faced, under any circumstances, with the unhappy task of supervising a spirited eight-year-old child. These are my policies:"

(Next comes the concluding material written by a member of the group.)

Step 7. Now compare what the class has written to the ineffective model we began with, asking students to discuss what they have learned through this exercise.

The emphasis in this exercise has been on the development of text. However, the process of development is also a process of revision. In the previous situation, individuals and groups were mostly inventing in the time they had and choosing among produced segments of narrative. Given more time, they may want to do some editing, too, combining the inventions of several students into a new composite segment that is better than any of the individual ones, perhaps shortening some parts while adding yet more detail to others. Or the class may want to revise the whole narrative, once they have heard it. They may want to eliminate inventions in the several segments that are too like each other, or make details fit together, or establish one tone for the whole narrative.

A family vacation in Disney World may not be a suitable topic for everyone. Other possibilities that the teacher may suggest include the following.

- Getting the groceries home while caring for a younger sister or brother.
- Securing agreement on which TV show a family of six will watch at 8:00 p.m.
- Learning to get along while working in a fast-food establishment.
- Having to balance earning money, dating, and doing homework.
- Trying to get tickets for a sold-out rock concert.

Reading

Discussion of readings in literature is an excellent vehicle for connecting the skills of reading, writing, listening, and speaking, but to illustrate strategies for connecting these skills we need texts we can display. For such texts we turn to two short poems and to long discussions of them, on several premises.

- The particular experience any work will give a student does not necessarily translate into another one, although experiences can and do accumulate, for better or worse.
- The *skills* of reading, however, do transfer from one experience to another.
- Poems to be used as instances of reading can be reprinted whole, and reading them asks for many of the same activities and perceptions needed for other genres.

The sample class plans that follow—in practice, a series of classes—are meant to apply to any kind of close reading. They are intended to engage students in a critical process—working on language by reading, talking, listening, and writing. Discussions of both poems focus on language: in the Langston Hughes poem on the mode of the sentences (questions which imply a statement) and on imagery; in the Richard Wilbur poem on imagery and allusion. In addition, suggested questions for the Hughes poem center on speaker and on audience response; suggested questions for the Wilbur poem on situation and on audience response. The order of presentation to a class would probably be the Hughes poem at an early stage of teaching close reading, the Wilbur poem at a later stage. In following the plan, teachers should bear in mind the generic questions about reading listed in Chapter 3. As they indicate, work in reading is not linear, a march down a straight road. It is recursive, returning to itself to encourage and improve skills by practicing them and to increase understanding by accumulating experience. We are always doing again in a different way what we have done before.

Plan I: A Reading Lesson

Begin Langston Hughes's poem without assignment, impromptu in class.

Harlem

What happens to a dream deferred?

> Does it dry up
> like a raisin in the sun?
> Or fester like a sore
> And then run?
>
> Does it stink like rotten meat?
> Or crust and sugar over
> like a syrupy sweet?
>
> Maybe it just sags
> like a heavy load.
>
> *Or does it explode?*[1]

Ask someone in the class to read the poem. Begin class discussion with questions about anything this reading suggests: words that give trouble, lines that do not follow. Then ask other questions.

- What is meant by a "dream deferred"? Is that a contradiction? How can a dream be deferred?
- Why the questions? Are they about alternatives?
- What feelings does the speaker suggest? Grief? Anger? Fright? Is the speaker menacing or being menaced?

One way to address these questions is in the group as a whole. Another is to divide the class into smaller groups, giving each of them one of the clusters of questions to consider and to report to the class about. One such report should reinforce another and should lead into general discussion of the whole poem.

The first set of questions may be puzzling to the group discussing them. What does it mean to defer something? How can a dream be set aside for some future time? Students talking together will work out that perhaps a dream itself—a condition in the mind—is not in the future, but fulfilling it can be. Yearning is not deferred, but fulfilling a dream can certainly be put off. Students will arrive at that distinction in various ways. Assure them then that they are right to make it; it is essential to the questions that follow.

---

1. Langston Hughes, "Harlem," from *The Panther and the Lash*, in *Selected Poems of Langston Hughes* (New York: Alfred A. Knopf, 1959), p. 199.

Take up the next group's report. Why does the speaker ask these questions? There is no one best answer. Students may suggest any of a number of possibilities.

- The speaker's rhetorical motives: a desire to involve listeners.
- Something to do with the speaker's emotional condition: a way to suggest his own involvement, or a way to sort out feelings and discover what they are.
- A sense of economy: the questions, though they are brief, suggest a variety of situations.

Are the questions about alternatives? Take a few minutes for consideration of what "alternatives" are, perhaps alluding to one set of alternatives: the list of possible answers to why the speaker asks questions. Make a list on the board of the words as the group refers to them: "dry up," "fester," "stink," "crust and sugar over," "sag," "explode." Do the students think these are alternatives to each other, different things that might happen?

Each of the first four images is a picture of a mental condition that the speaker imagines, each one distasteful, even revolting. The third group of students, who are working on the feelings that are suggested, should have several answers: grief, anger, and fright are implied by the images. But whether the speaker is menacing or menaced is harder to answer, for the series of questions is like a sequence in the mind, and the speaker may be implying both.

Out of the several reports the class may construct a dramatic situation: the speaker in the poem is someone whose alternatives are all bad. They add up to a general effect that is also expressed as an image—the heavy load of weariness, of emotional exhaustion. But they also add up to an alternative general effect. When he mentions an explosion, is the speaker still talking about something inside the mind? Discussion of this question will probably include both metaphorical and literal readings. Teachers may want to place it in a context, however, either to explain or—if the students already know—to ask the class to provide information about other displays of anger in black communities and in New York's Harlem as one of those communities. Someone may then wonder if the title stands for a particular event that took place at a specific time. Someone else may suggest that the place of action continues to be inside the speaker's mind, but the emotion suggested is rage, not despair. Another may add that whether the literal place or the metaphorical place "Harlem" is meant, it could be community anger, group anger, not private, individual anger the question refers to. In that case, we might ask, what does Harlem represent? Would "explode" be a good thing? Is the speaker suggesting it would?

In discussing such a set of questions, a class works toward an understanding of a poem. Understanding includes its paraphrasable content, but discussion demonstrates how a reader arrives at that content. Readers discover for themselves that the early questions in the poem become frightening, threatening, or attractive because the speaker is making a statement through those questions. The poem's questions are challenging the reader to face something, to take a position about something. The poem has power and strength when all the parts are understood and put together. Make some such explicit conclusion for the class, as a conscious review of what the discussion has accomplished, and to underline that their talk had a purpose. Before class ends, ask someone to read the poem aloud again.

Presentation of this poem starts impromptu in one class period. But completing it will take at least two class sessions. An informal writing assignment such as the following might link the two discussions:

Directions: For class tomorrow, write down in your journal what we have learned so far about the poem.

Using this informal writing, vary the format of the first day. Ask students to read their responses, letting where they are in their reading of the poem direct the second discussion. Such a procedure suggests that writing is a tool for remembering and understanding, and can be a preliminary to sharing. The content of what is written also directs attention to listening and speaking: How much did you hear and remember? What did you say as a participant and how did others understand it?

Or use a more formal writing assignment to follow up discussion. For a paper written over several days, outside class, the following topic might be used.

Directions: Hughes's poem "Harlem" talks about "a dream deferred." Think about your own plans for your life so far. Explain to the class whether there is a dream deferred for you or for someone you know well. You may take either position—that there is not, because you have done and are doing things you want to, or that there is. In either case give us enough explanation so that we will understand what the situation is that you are describing and how you feel about it.

For a paper written in class, the topic might be given out in advance so that students can prepare to write, but it should call for a shorter response.

Directions: Think back over our discussion of Hughes's poem "Harlem." Write a paper in which you explain for the class why the effects it describes of deferring a dream make you feel frightened for yourself, or make you want to do something to change them, or produce a combination of feelings that you would not describe in either of those ways.

Plan II: A Second Reading Lesson

The discussion of the following poem is a sample for students who have had earlier experience in understanding and talking about poems. It is an instance of richly allusive language that rewards close study.

The Death of a Toad
by Richard Wilbur

A toad the power mower caught,
Chewed and clipped of a leg, with a hobbling hop has got
  To the garden verge, and sanctuaried him
  Under the cineraria leaves, in the shade
    Of the ashen heartshaped leaves, in a dim,
      Low, and a final glade.

The rare original heartsblood goes,
Spends on the earthen hide, in the folds and wizenings, flows
  In the gutters of the banked and staring eyes. He lies
  As still as if he would return to stone,
    And soundlessly attending, dies
      Toward some deep monotone,

> Toward misted and ebullient seas
> And cooling shores, toward lost Amphibia's emperies.
> Day dwindles, drowning, and at length is gone
> In the wide and antique eyes, which still appear
> To watch, across the castrate lawn,
> The haggard daylight steer.[2]

Ask someone in the class to read the whole poem aloud. If the reading suggests a particular place to start, start there. In any case, move to the poem's most basic level of meaning by asking what it is about—that is, what happens in the poem. The following should emerge: a toad's leg is injured by a power mower; the toad goes to the edge of the lawn and dies; in death, the toad still appears to be staring across the lawn.

Students will generally be dissatisfied with this simple "story" of the poem. They will ask—or the teacher should—"What else is the poem about?" Part of the answer to this question lies in the study of language.

A good starting point is the word "sanctuaried." On being questioned, a student might observe that the word means more than simply safe—it has a religious connotation. Or someone might observe that churches have sanctuaries, or might mention someone seeking sanctuary. While none of these comments is exactly to the point, each justifies the sense that the poem is about something beyond the death of a garden toad. "Cineraria" is another word to call attention to. Looking it up in a dictionary, students may find a definition close to the words Wilbur uses in the next line: a bush having ashen, heartshaped leaves. The teacher might ask, "Why would a poet use what is essentially a dictionary definition of a word?" Students can learn that the poet may be heavily underlining a reference. Here is a garden plant that draws its name from the ash-colored down on its leaves, a name very like a name of the place—the cinerarium—holding the ashes of the dead. Thus, in two instances, students see that close study of the words reinforces the idea that the poem is about more than its surface subject. The level of thought and study within the poem has been raised. The

---

2. Richard Wilbur, "The Death of a Toad," from *Ceremony and Other Poems*, in *The Poems of Richard Wilbur* (New York: Harcourt, Brace & World, 1967), p. 152.

study of other individual words ("ebullient," "castrate," "haggard") further reinforces the idea.

Line 10 contains the clause "as if he would return to stone." But when was the toad stone before? The question may be raised by students or by the teacher. Answers—in terms of the origin of life, the beginnings of existence—may be very vague: "Isn't there some theory that stones gradually wear down into dirt? Is it like the idea that man began from dust? Does it suggest something about before life began?" Once this lead is given, attention can shift to such phrases as "earthen hide," "lost Amphibia's emperies," "ebullient seas/And cooling shores." Students begin to realize that (1) the implications of the words are relevant considerations, and (2) this poem is asking us to think about a time before the presence of humans.

The poem's implications have now broadened to a question of beginnings, as well as of a tiny death. Students may be puzzled. Why call in such a broad area? Yet careful discussion may suggest that it is the other way around: Wilbur may have been interested in the toad because it is a survivor of an earlier age. The point to emphasize is the inseparable relationship between the two—the particular event of the death of the toad and the far-reaching things we become aware of through the language telling us about it.

In the last stanza the dead toad's eyes are staring out of "Amphibia's emperies" at a dying world: "To watch, across the castrate lawn/The haggard daylight steer." Amphibia's emperies: "Amphibia" is a zoological term, the name of the class of vertebrates that toads belong to, another use of a dictionary definition, a technical word to which connotations of the ancient, faraway, glamorous are attached by its link with "emperies," a word for a wide domain of great power. In the context of the poem that lost place is juxtaposed with man's present empery, the dominated space where the power mower is castrating the lawn. We may ask, "What are the implications of these descriptions? Are the worlds like or unlike each other?"

At this point we might reflect on students' experiences in a reading like this. They have carefully read three stanzas of poetry in which the poet has taken them from a small event, the death of a lowly toad, to a consideration of the origins of life and an implied question about human survival. They have observed closely, commented on, and assessed the parts that make up the whole. But their study should not be left as an experience of parts. Ask someone to read the poem again.

Several kinds of writing can grow out of such discussions. The first day that the poem is read, ask students to take five minutes to write in their journals.

Directions: Now that you have read the poem yourself and heard it read aloud, just write for five minutes about your instant, personal response. What is it? How do you feel about this poem? Can you connect any of your feelings to anything in particular in the poem?

Ask students to put their journal entries aside while everyone talks about the poem. There may be allusions to what is in the entries, but do not ask students to read or defend them.

At the end of class, make the following assignment to be done at home.

Directions: Write in your journal your reactions to the poem now. Write fast. What you are doing is discussing the poem with yourself as you get ready to read it aloud to the class tomorrow. Now decide how you would read the poem.

In class next day, ask for volunteers to read the poem aloud. Take time for several people to read the poem. Ask the class, as prepared listeners, what they noticed about the poem as they listened to it. Start discussion of the poem from there.

At the end of class discussion of the poem, make a further assignment.

Directions: Look up at least two dictionary definitions of another of the words in Wilbur's poem. Write a paper for the rest of us in which you assume that no one else has looked up that word. Explain how its meanings add to an understanding of the poem.

Other Reading Plans

Students should also learn the skills of skimming, selecting, and isolating what to read carefully, of noting what is found, and of remembering it. In teaching straightforward factual materials—for instance, that Shakespeare, Milton, Flaubert, Dickinson, Woolf, Ellison (choose your own list) lived in different times from each other—ask the class to read about the writers and find out for themselves. Send them in search of information, perhaps breaking the list of writers into assignments to individual students, who then report to the whole group, or dividing the class into groups responsible for a longer list of writers, each group concentrating on writers from a different time. Have students prepare a timetable with names and titles. The group then receives and shares information, noting it for later use. At the same time, members of the class are demonstrating by what they report that long sources of information can be reduced to the shorter report of facts. The fact that what has been gathered can be set up as a table or list also demonstrates skimming, gleaning, and recording what is wanted. To use the material that has been gathered, we may ask students to memorize; and then we may review and test. If we want the dates to stay with students longer than the day of the test, we use them in following classes, and we demonstrate by these uses why the dates are important.

Point out in discussion other activities that reading demands. Ask students to distinguish the way they read to find and record facts from the way they read a novel or short story. Among other things, students may notice that narrative reading drives itself along. They are aware of curiosity about plot, about character, about the idea behind it all. Or they may notice that with the text of a play, the activity of reading takes on another dimension. A reader works out a kind of mental staging from the speeches and stage directions on a page and makes more explicit something that the text only gives clues for.

Encourage students to see likenesses as well as differences in kinds of reading. Sometimes, with narrative, a reader pauses over allusions and images as if the text were a poem; sometimes in reading a poem it is situation and a sense of someone there telling about it, as the narrator of a novel does, that occupies attention. An awareness of likenesses and differences among the genres is something that can give pleasure, and also something readers can use in their own writing, transferring analytical skills to their own creation of text.

In such activities, it is plain that Basic Academic Competencies interlock. Those competencies also add up to a particular kind of studying—the study of language, what it does, how it works, what its uses are—and include certainty that study depends on the presence and use of reasoning skills. As we examine how language works we are seeing and stating positions or hypotheses, looking for the evidence that supports or challenges them, modifying them, fitting them in place among other hypotheses, and making judgments.

Asking Questions: Some Additional Thoughts

We ask questions, but not because English is an "answer" subject. For instance, there are no absolute answers to the following questions.

- What is the best format for a personal statement to accompany a college entrance application?
- Why is "fragrance" a better choice of word in some contexts than "odor"?
- What does *Hamlet* mean?

We may arrive at good answers to these questions but not definitive ones. It is the attitude of *seeking* answers, not of fastening on them, that we try to communicate to our students by the classroom methods we use. We want student dialogue, the opportunity to grow intellectually and imaginatively, which is given by talking, writing, testing ideas, reacting to others, and experimenting with words.

Questions are useful when they recognize that most of us learn little the first time we encounter something new, particularly in intellectual matters. We need to come back several times, question in several ways, before we make real progress. In a new situation good questions use terms we have heard before and ask that the familiar be applied to the unknown, the not yet thought. Such repetition provides a genuine opportunity to come at things, to become proficient in one's approach to understanding.

Encouraging a Discussion

How do we encourage all students to answer questions, to take part in discussions? In part, by the reception we provide for what they say.

Theodore Sizer mentions in *Horace's Compromise*[3] the excellent teacher who remembers and refers to students' contributions to a discussion and who makes use of what they have said. A habit of doing this—giving a student credit by name—is useful in two ways. It encourages further discussion by showing respect for ideas and information, making each student feel that what he or she says is worth saying, and it provides an example for students to respond to one another.

In the abstract, we say we respect student response. In the classroom, we may be abrupt and impatient. Students who customarily receive negative reactions to their replies are being conditioned to failure. Dealing with that is a teacher's dilemma in any subject. The subject of English seems especially tricky, for there are not very often single "right" answers, yet there are answers that are wrong—misstatement of fact, distorted reading, misunderstanding of what is being said. We can correct errors of fact. We can promote clarification; we can make sure a question was understood; we can draw the speaker out (sometimes) to a reading that takes more account of the text because we have asked more questions about it; we can recall something this student said earlier that does fit in now.

Or we can take time in class when we ask a question for discussion to give each student a chance to prepare and write down an answer, then call for answers from students who seldom volunteer. We can divide the class into groups, and this time, instead of being sure there is an active student in each group, put the quiet ones together. The usually silent will need to talk with each other within the group; and when the groups report, at least one will be speaking to the whole class. Our own awareness of individual students is one key; another is providing situations in which each one can and does talk.

Assignment and Test Questions

There are many ways other than class discussion that we use questions. Study questions can accompany assignments: here are

---

3. Theodore R. Sizer, *Horace's Compromise: The Dilemma of the American High School* (Boston: Houghton Mifflin, 1984), pp. 43-45.

the topics we will start with in class tomorrow; these are questions to think about as you begin our new novel; have these questions in mind as you work on your paper.

Questions are often the basis of the papers we assign and the essay examinations we give. We aim for variety, not just of subject matter but also of form: some factual questions, some open-ended questions. Some questions will be based on a text open before the student; some on a text that must be remembered; some on several texts pulled together; some on personal experience informed by reading; some on personal experience alone. In deciding the level of sophistication and the appropriateness of questions, we relate the questions—for ourselves and for our students—to the purposes of a unit, course, or curriculum.

We also include questions that allow for a variety of response. We want all students to be able to respond effectively in the traditional modes of written examinations. But we can provide opportunities to demonstrate knowledge and skills in other ways: journals, oral presentations, group projects, artistic representations, dramatizations, films. In providing varied outlets for expression we are (1) recognizing our responsibilities to help our students develop in a variety of ways, (2) providing legitimate outlets for demonstrating knowledge and skill, (3) acknowledging the richness of human diversity, and (4) fostering integration of multiple skills.

V. English and the Basic Academic Competencies

We want much for our students as they leave high school. We hope that they have the feeling of a special moment, a time of important tasks completed, of competence gathered to meet challenges and opportunities yet to come. We want them to have learned and to know how to learn again. But, of course, such is not always the case. Some students will come to this moment with the sense of time merely passed or wasted; others will lack an inward grasp of how they got where they are or of what it means to go forward. Perhaps most will feel some puzzle within themselves. High school days, as they unfold, are not as definite as we might like, but rather are sometimes volatile, felt alternately as bright or cruel, always alive with change.

Effective teachers do not seek to quell change, but rather attempt to tap its energy and to encourage the learning that can give it purpose and depth. In the Green Book other teachers set forth the academic competencies students most need to approach their futures with confidence: reading, writing, speaking and listening, mathematics, reasoning, studying, using computers, and observing. Students can do much with these skills, both for themselves and for others; but we do not mean to say that possession of these skills, even to a very marked degree, puts an end to all uncertainty or reduces the suspense students feel about the future.

In uncertainty, however, there is the potential, the very ground, for search and for achievement in finding one's way. As Henry James said, it "seems probable that if we were never bewildered there would never be a story to tell about us."[1] In making outcomes

---

1. Henry James, Preface to *The Princess Casamassima*, in *The Art of the Novel*, R. P. Blackmur, ed. (New York: Charles Scribner's Sons, 1934), p. 63.

explicit, we do not presume that students can become superior, all-knowing achievers. These outcomes will not exist in perfection in any actual situation, and the effort to achieve them will not reduce the human flurry. We will always have moments of success and failure, loss and gain, days that are interesting and days that are dull. All these things are part of what happens when teachers and students become part of one another's story for a time. What should not happen is that questions that arise from bewilderment, questions that may inspire or plague, recede into a kind of blankness. If making desired learning outcomes explicit does anything, it should imply that questions have a future and that knowledge, with competence in using it, keeps that future open, complex, and bright with promise.

Later in this chapter, we will describe learning situations in which students have the kind of classroom experience that can lead to acquisition of the Basic Academic Competencies. At the outset, though, we want to make two points.

1. The term competence, for some, implies something narrow or purely technical. We intend no such meaning. Our competence is no less than ourselves, a valuable part of our identity and strength. The class exercises we will discuss are small and seemingly limited; however, we believe that they carry within themselves the potential for fundamental growth.

2. Moreover, we do not think of the competencies as something "added on" to coverage of academic subject matter. Rather, they are acquired and take on reality through pursuit of the questions we ask of subject matter. The teacher's questions both point students to the issues in a subject area and elicit from them the development (or use) of skills necessary if they are to become active participants in engaging these issues.

Literature, Competence, and Self

The range of academic outcomes cited in the Green Book reflects the complexity of modern life. Our literature, which is itself so various, often reflects a concern that this complexity is too much for us, that the center cannot hold. In teaching, therefore, our subject matter brings us again and again to this concern and to the very personal ways in which our students feel it. Santayana wrote that the dilemma of the life of reason was whether it must sacrifice natural abundance to order, or order to natural abundance. "Whatever compromise we choose," he wrote, "proves unstable, and forces us to a new experiment."[2]

We may not phrase this condition exactly as Santayana did, but we probably agree that the tension exists—that the relation between the number of outcomes and the need to integrate them is a dynamic one, a matter that we neither can nor wish to settle easily. Perhaps we can also agree that our efforts in the direction of integration are more in the nature of experiments than prescriptions. They are, that is, acts we subject to trial and test, not certainties that we deliver by rote and rule. In this important sense, the study of English shares the same outlook as the other Basic Academic Subjects, the same spirit of quest and flexibility; and to understand this is also to begin to grasp how all of study comes together and acts with common purpose.

In achieving competence in reading and writing, we English teachers have recourse to the vast resources of imaginative literature. Consideration of this body of work reminds us that the material we teach is itself a vital element in the dynamic (and dramatic) relation between abundance and order, variety and integration. Lionel Trilling has observed that literature teaches us, as nothing else does, the extent of human variety and the value of this variety. In teaching, therefore, we find ourselves immersed in material that resists the closed view, the narrow approach, to ideas and issues. It places value on fullness, complexity, and possibility. These values, in turn, are absorbed into the sense of competence in reading and writing that we seek with our students. We try to help them develop and practice these competencies, not as technical skills solely, but as the large human powers that they are.

---

2. George Santayana, *The Intellectual Temper of the Age*, in *Selected Critical Writings of George Santayana* (Cambridge, England: Cambridge University Press, 1968), p. 9.

Doubtless, this is part of the explanation for our misgivings about uniform reading lists. These reduce a field that must remain large, various, and open to renewal and revision. Indeed, as a practical matter, there is no high school curriculum that can put an end to the shocked response by our college colleagues that student preparation has not included the reading of this or that particular text. Preferences of college faculties are too various to suppose that everyone, or most, could ever be satisfied. Probably this is a healthy situation and keeps us on our toes in the selection of readings, even if it does not provide definite guidance. What is more important, however, is that students attend closely to a variety of literary texts and come to know them well enough to grasp the elements that give them order within themselves. This includes, for example, the aspects that make up a literary voice such as tone, nuance, and rhythm. Once students are alert to such elements, and add them to their reading competence, they will be able to see how a text acquires form and has integrity within itself. Moreover, if these same elements can then be noted in texts studied later in other settings, students become able at the same time to integrate readings and to distinguish their different shades and intentions.

If the formal integrity of a work of literature is to be found within itself, it is also true that its power to bond is in something that happens between text and reader. This has to do with the fact that the voice of literature is almost always personal. While it intends to do justice to a subject or a theme, it also seeks to affect the reader, to reach the self. We must remember that, while literary texts are discussed in the classroom, they are intended to be read and experienced in privacy.

Students react in kind to the personal intensity of literature and find its meaning in reference to their own lives. In consequence, the same devotion to personal truth, to what a text means for one's self, may be sought from the teacher. With some mixed feelings, Trilling wrote, "Nowadays the teaching of literature inclines to a considerable technicality, but when the teacher has said what can be said about formal matters, about verse-patterns, metrics, prose connections, irony, tensions, etc., he must confront the necessity of bearing personal testimony. He must use whatever authority he may possess to say whether or not a work is true; and if not, why not; and if so, why so. He can do this only at considerable cost to his privacy."[3] Teachers will know where and how they stand on this matter, and they will come to it in different ways at different times in the classroom. The critical point is that literature addresses its questions to the self, and, in doing so, does not ask for received opinion or the accepted position, but rather how the reader arrives at his or her own view. The necessity to take this personal ground in reading and writing, and to know how one has found it, can be a vital contributive force in the integration of mind and identity.

Transfer

This is not to say, of course, that reading and writing only deal with the personal and inward. They are also the competencies through which we try to understand and express ourselves to the world and to others. In the practice of reading and writing students reach out and in, enter into the interdependence of things, and acquire a sense of relation and effectiveness.

To assist these recognitions, teachers of English can guide students in exercises that involve, either explicitly or implicitly, the transfer of competence in reading and writing to the development of other knowledge and skills. These exercises can be simple in conception, but they still reverberate across the curriculum and throughout the time students spend in school.

For example, one teacher asks students to read a short excerpt from Alfred Kazin's autobiographical work, *A Walker in the City*[4]— the brief section dealing with the kitchen in the Brownsville tenement home of his childhood (reproduced in Appendix A). As the reader can see, Kazin shows how this room—a place and setting— shaped and revealed the special character of his own life, that of his family, and of an immigrant culture. He does this not through argument or large generalization, but through close, precise atten-

---

3. Lionel Trilling, "On the Teaching of Modern Literature," in *Beyond Culture* (New York: Viking, 1955), p. 9.

4. Alfred Kazin, *A Walker in the City* (New York and London: Harcourt Brace Jovanovich, 1951), pp. 64-71.

tion to the interaction between material fact and the development of human thought and feeling. We see much, for instance, of how place and person come together when we follow Kazin's description of the light in the room, the paint on the walls, and the sounds from the street. It is in the absorption of such things within himself that Kazin grew as a sentient human being.

This is an exercise, first of all, in the interdependence of reading and writing. After considering the Kazin passages, students can be asked to identify and write about a place or setting that has had a bearing on their own lives similar to that of the kitchen in Kazin's. This is more than autobiographical writing; it is what might be called a cultural consideration of one's life. It is directed not to self alone, but to the joinings of identity, place, and culture. As with Kazin, intimations of history also will emerge. The point, however, is not to be overly directive in discussing these connections. Students should experience the pleasant recognition that *reading* about Kazin's Brooklyn can lead them to *writing* about a spot in Texas, or Los Angeles, or along the Ohio River. This perhaps makes the somewhat abstract point that power in reading and writing grows as each acts and reacts on the other. For students, it also will provide a quickening sense of how these competencies at once take one within oneself and span great differences in culture and experience. They are transferred between reading and writing, from one world to another.

The purpose, moreover, is not for the student to write "like" or "as well as" Kazin. Indeed, the pressure to do either of these things must be minimized. One can speak of the Kazin passage as a model, but it is more appropriate to think of it as an inspiration or catalyst. The point is not to give students a pattern to trace, but rather to introduce them to a ground that will support them in making their own way. Class discussion can touch on the "how" of what Kazin has done, but the teacher may want to keep this relatively simple. For example, the passages afford many opportunities to emphasize the relation between fact and metaphor (for example, the way in which the sewing machine is both material thing and idea). However, steadfast attention to the writer's commitment to telling detail reveals how familiar material things and human meaning shade into one another after long association. Metaphor, then, often takes care of itself.

Indeed, the intention is not to give large amounts of class time to discussion of Kazin, but rather to focus on the written products of the students. As many as possible should be shared through class reading and discussion; and here full attention should be given to how tellingly and interestingly students render the fact and spirit of a chosen place. In this discussion the competencies of speaking and listening described in Chapter 2 come into play, giving students a good opportunity to practice and recognize how these skills build on and add to the work of reading and writing. Many teachers who have used this exercise, or some version of it, have remarked on the increased interplay of language skills it brings into the classroom. Not that there is frequent interruption to say, "this is where skill acts on skill," but through it all can be felt a flow of the read, the written, the spoken, and the heard.

The Kazin passages also point to the interplay among reading, writing, and the competency of observing. One cannot consider this writing without noting how it is grounded, with the aid of memory, in close and precise observation. Here, for example, is part of his look around the kitchen.

> The walls were a fiercely stippled whitewash, so often rewhitened by my father in slack seasons that the paint looked as if it had been squeezed and cracked into the walls. A large electric bulb hung down the center of the kitchen at the end of a chain that had been hooked into the ceiling; the old gas ring and key still jutted out of the wall like antlers. In the corner next to the toilet was the sink at which we washed, and the square tub in which my mother did our clothes. Above it, tacked to the shelf on which were pleasantly ranged square, blue-bordered white sugar and spice jars, hung calendars from the Public National Bank on Pitkin Avenue and the Minsker Progressive Branch of the Workman's Circle; receipts for the payment of insurance premiums, and household bills on a spindle; two little boxes engraved with Hebrew letters.[5]

From attention to textual material of this kind, students grow to recognize that writing does not come from a void or depend on things of which they have no knowledge. Rather, it begins with

---

5. Kazin, pp. 65-66.

close observation of the things nearest them, the mysteries of the familiar. We teach how the impressions of the alert eye and competency in observing can be transferred and enlarged in power through competency in writing and reading.

This emphasis on what is actually in front of one's eye, and on all that is there to be seen, may be a necessary antidote to a prejudice our culture sometimes harbors against literature. Teachers encounter the feeling that the readings of the English classroom are a collection of "not so" stories. This is partly because literature partakes of imagination and so can come to be regarded as "unreal" or "untrue." While this is a complicated matter, teachers of English must remind students of the fact that serious literature is not about "making things up." The source of good writing, including that of a student, is most naturally to be found in looking around oneself and in seeing things for what they are and for all they are worth. In this connection, it may help to acquaint students with what one of our greatest imaginative writers says about the relation of the writing craft to observation of the real. Ralph Ellison has spoken of how he grew in his own writing competence through reading the work of other writers. Hemingway was particularly important, not only because he wrote of courage in the face of impossible circumstances, but also because he called the young writer's attention to the importance of carefully observing "the things of this earth." In making this point, Ellison says that Hemingway wrote "with such precision about the processes and techniques of daily living that I could keep myself and my brother alive during the 1937 Recession by following his descriptions of wing-shooting. . . ."[6] Ellison does not mean, of course, that Hemingway had written a manual about how to shoot game birds. Rather, he intends to call attention to the fact that serious literature focuses its eye on the true, rendering it real and exact.

Ellison's reference to how he learned from Hemingway conveys the writing process discussed in Chapter 3. In this, observing is the departure for prewriting. One can imagine the steps Hemingway

---

6. Ralph Ellison, "The World and the Jug," in *Shadow and Act* (New York: New American Library, 1953), p. 145.

must have taken and completed, even if his movement through them was idiosyncratic: (1) observing others and himself in the act of wing-shooting, (2) thinking through its elements as seen and experienced, (3) writing, (4) rereading to see if the writing enabled the audience to see, experience, and think through the subject in the way intended.

Observing activities can produce good prewriting exercises. Ask students to think for a moment about how often in literature we are given the thoughts and feelings of major characters as they look from a window toward some outside scene. Kazin, for instance, closes the picture of his mother (in the passages excerpted) with her looking from a window at the gathering dusk and the still-crowded street below. It can be interesting to ask what this is all about. Why so many windows in literature? Why so much looking out? To increase students' sense of the question, ask them to look through a window divided into several panes. First, have them write a brief paragraph (a list, if it is more appropriate) describing what they see. Then, have them look through one pane at a time, writing a description (or list) of what they observe through each. (If students start with lists these develop readily into paragraphs in a next stage.) Comparison of the two observations can lead discussions in many different directions: consideration of detail versus broad impressions; matters of scale, framing, or point of view. Most will permit students to experience some of the delights and surprises of observation and, at the same time, acquaint them with the gains of the prewriting step.

We might also consider how this exercise involves competency in reasoning. Much is said throughout this book about reasoning. It would not be possible, nor would it serve any purpose, to attempt a summary at this point or to follow all the pedagogical implications through in suggested practice. Perhaps we can agree, in any case, that reason is the inescapable commitment of our classrooms and that it enters into almost everything that we do as teachers.

As an instance, take one function of reasoning listed in the Green Book: the "ability to identify and formulate problems, as well as the ability to propose and evaluate ways to solve them." How might this aspect of competence be approached in the window pane exercise decribed previously? Suppose a timed activity. Suggest that students clock themselves or each other while looking out of a window. What does each see in a 20- or 30-second "look"? Have them write it down and share it with classmates. Then ask if students have "seen" differently. This may at first seem only a matter of count, some students having longer lists than others. Here one can ask if number is the only way to identify and formulate questions of difference. From this, different configurations of observing usually emerge. Students not only will have different lists, but also will recognize that they have seen in different ways and begin to propose groupings for formulating the distinctions (details/ vista, people/things, color/shapes, definition/descriptions).

Several competency interests are served at once as this work goes forward. The prewriting exercise is extended by asking students to think through what they have observed. Speaking and listening skills are emphasized again as students collaborate in discussing the lists. And students practice reasoning skills as they identify and formulate the problem of "difference" among the lists. It is almost certain that the formulation of the questions will change several times over the course of the discussion, involving experience in evaluation and sharpening the sense of problem solving. Students, for example, may become skeptical that a longer list is necessarily the better one. On the other hand, they also will see the difficulty in identifying one "best" way of seeing. In so doing they may begin to grasp the challenge of bringing order to variety, and variety to order, which Santayana identified as the creative tension at the center of the life of reason.

Mathematics

The foregoing discussion dealt with transfer of skills within English classrooms. What is involved, though, when we seek to transfer them to other classrooms? Here we will offer a few suggestions using the competencies of reading and mathematics as illustrations. On the surface these two competencies may seem to be entirely separate; they are often treated as such. But we know that many students have difficulty reading mathematical textbooks, and this is likely to be diagnosed as poorly developed reading skills. When help is provided, it often consists of returning the student to the English teacher for remedial instruction in basic word recognition and literal comprehension. The underlying idea seems to be that if a certain set of basic reading skills is mastered in the English class, comprehension will take care of itself in other academic subject areas.

This "deficit" theory of reading instruction is inadequate to the problem. It labels as "problem readers" students who may instead need experience transferring their skills to the language needs of a new subject matter. This is true for all the Basic Academic Subjects. High school textbooks in all subject areas present students with vocabulary in a context where skill in pronouncing an unfamiliar word will often not establish its meaning. Recognition of meaning depends on experience, and students who lack experience with concepts discussed will not be able to make much sense of the discussion, no matter how well developed their basic word-decoding skills are.

The limitations of the deficit model in reading are similar to the limitations of the deficit model in mathematics: students identified as deficient in basic skills are recycled through remedial instruction designed to teach these skills, when their real need is to develop both skills and understanding in the context of interesting new content. Students are labeled as deficient—which sets up a self-reinforcing set of expectations about their performance—and instruction is then aimed in the negative direction of overcoming their weaknesses rather than building on their strengths.

Nelson-Herber and Herber argue that "the majority of students who seem to need corrective reading instruction in middle and secondary schools don't." Their argument rests on the conviction

> that all students should have the benefit of reading instruction in every classroom where reading is required, and that reading strategies should be taught simultaneously with the content of the subject being taught. If this were done, very few students would need corrective instruction. Unfortunately, we generally abandon the teaching of reading at the very point where students need to integrate the skills gleaned from basic reading instruction with their knowledge, their experience and their reasoning power to address more complex reading comprehension tasks.

Some students, of course, need corrective reading instruction. But that instruction should be designed to complement reading instruction that is conducted in the mathematics classroom itself.[7]

Mathematics textbooks provide rich material for reading instruction. Much of the exposition is dense with new ideas and terminology. Students can write alternative versions in their own words and, by reading one another's work, clarify difficult points. Some teachers have found that having students write their own versions of textbook word problems—as well as having them make up their own problems (as in the "Pizza to Go" vignette in Chapter 4 of *Academic Preparation in Mathematics*)—alerts them to how problems are phrased and how meaning can be changed by a slight rewording.

Because so many students have difficulty reading mathematical material, some textbook writers have attempted to minimize the extent and reading level of the English prose in mathematics books. The prose becomes a sort of Pidgin English. The hope of these writers seems to be that the textbook is thereby rendered easier to use—easier, that is, for the student who does not want to read but only wants an illustration of how to work the exercises in the book. When working exercises is the primary goal, a book with a minimum amount of exposition allows a lot of room for exercises. But if understanding the ideas behind the exercises is the goal, there is no way—and no reason—to avoid using clear English sentences that convey the ideas, illustrating them and providing a context for them. Fortunately, more mathematics textbooks are beginning to appear in which the English language is used to examine, illustrate, explain, and discuss rather than merely to point.

We should remember that mathematics is a language—or, better said, mathematics is a collection of languages. Each of these languages is more specialized than a natural language such as English. Reading a mathematical argument, therefore, requires skills in

---

7. Joan Nelson-Herber and Harold L. Herber, "A Positive Approach to Assessment and Correction of Reading Difficulties in Middle and Secondary Schools." In *Promoting Reading Comprehension*, James Flood, ed. (Newark, Delaware: International Reading Association, 1984), p. 234.

close reading—in making every symbol count. Mathematics teachers need to help students appreciate the nature of mathematical language by showing them how slight alterations have drastic consequences. Computer programming provides an excellent context for illustrating this point. Students readily come to appreciate that computers are ordinarily very unforgiving when they are addressed incorrectly in one of the common programming languages. A student quickly learns that a misplaced semicolon or a misspelled word stops the computer cold. Mathematics teachers can point out that the same attention that is given to each symbol in writing a computer program ought to be given to each symbol in reading a mathematical text. The teacher of English might make this same point by reference to poetry.

Computer Competency

Teachers of English, like most of their colleagues, are only beginning to develop ideas about the place of computers in the school curriculum. Where these ideas will lead depends on several things, not the least of which are changes in technology and decisions about the allocations of resources. The word processor already is having some influence on the way writing is done, if not yet very much on how writing is learned; and its availability as a means requires our attention in order that we understand better how it can help our ends.

One question is availability. Some students have access to computers through school centers: a few fortunate students may own personal computers. Where there is such possibility, teachers can build units and lessons that encourage computer skill development, particularly as it applies to the writing process. Students can be encouraged to see how word processing speeds revisions by eliminating the need for recopying or the nuisance of cutting and pasting. Word processing programs permit a writer to revise words, sentences, or segments at will, and they make it easy to move text from one place to another. Their split-screen device makes it possible not only to look at two versions of a piece of writing at once but to transfer text from one to the other. They provide good-looking final copy when the revisions are completed. All of these possibilities can encourage a writer's efforts by increasing the sense of control and command. That command is over the machine, not over the writing process; but at least the prospective writer can focus on the creative elements of writing and not be put off by the mechanical repetitions that can impede writing.

In schools that have computer centers, teachers can devise interesting writing exercises. If there are personal computers available to whole classes, we can ask students to compare two versions of a piece of writing by means of the split screen, and everyone can work, simultaneously or sequentially, on revising the text. If the personal computers are connected with each other, students can exchange papers electronically, and thus can make suggestions about changes in the text while retaining a copy of the original text in the writer's file. If the teacher, too, is using a terminal, messages back and forth with students are possible, and so is communication on general matters of class business.

We know that computers and their possibilities are a part of our future. English teachers who understand computing, and who give thought to its classroom applications, will be among those who shape this future. While we cannot foresee results, or feel as comfortable with computing as we do with other competencies, we know that it is now part of the field of vision and must be given increased attention.

VI. Toward Further Discussion

This is a small book. Given the scope of the subject and the relatively few pages available to address it, we have not thought to be either comprehensive in our treatment or definitive about an agenda for the future. Either of these intentions, in any case, would have been inconsistent with our major purpose. We have sought to deepen discussion about how to achieve desired outcomes, not to prescribe what conclusions should be drawn or to say what action must be taken. Some readers may be disappointed that we have not issued guidelines or made pointed recommendations. But we do not believe that most of our fellow teachers want such prescriptions. Those who teach in the high schools of America, public and private, know that desirable change comes, if it comes, through close engagement of questions in local settings. We look to outside sources for help, but finally the result depends on the things we make and do among ourselves.

In the course of preparing this book, we have observed a number of in-service days involving groups of English teachers as well as concerned and interested school administrators. Draft chapters of this book were considered and debated, but discussion did not fasten on right or wrong, agreement and disagreement. Rather, it turned toward how the suggestions made could be related to practice in particular schools and classrooms—and how they might help all involved to refresh their thinking about what currently happens in the teaching of English. Throughout, of course, there was a return to the question of how what was said argued either for or against what is now being done. In responding, teachers and administrators added to our statement from their own experience, usually making this a larger, more nearly complete, somewhat different book in doing so. That is what we wanted. The value of the book, we believe, is precisely in the fact that it does not seek to have the last word or to make the most eloquent remark. Instead, this book takes for itself the responsibility of speaking first, of opening the subject, and in so doing trusts that teachers will continue the dialogue.

Discussion in working sessions among colleagues may, and probably should, take up issues that we either have not addressed or have touched on all too briefly. Some of these issues may bear only indirectly on achieving the desired outcomes but are still vital in the making of the kind of learning situations we want. Others appear in this book but have not received the attention that they deserve. We will deal with a few such issues that we know are on the minds of our fellow teachers: numbers and time, collaboration between schools and colleges, writing across the curriculum, and asking questions.

Numbers and Time

We spoke earlier about the problems of numbers and time. In most schools there simply are too many classes in the day and too many students in each class. The consequence is that the time we have to give to important tasks is much too small. There *is* growing recognition of the seriousness of this problem. In drawing the portrait of an experienced, conscientious high school English teacher, Theodore Sizer writes:

> Most jobs in the real world have a gap between what would be nice and what is possible. One adjusts. The tragedy for many high school teachers is that the gap is a chasm, not crossed by reasonable and judicious adjustments. Even after adroit accommodations and devastating compromises—only *five minutes per week* of attention on the written work of each student and an average of ten minutes of planning for each fifty-odd minute class—the task is already crushing, in reality a sixty-hour week.[1]

The problem is not just lack of time but the fact that the time we have is divided into small units. There is no fluency or flow of time, and this undercuts the sense of continuity in learning. Our sched-

---

1. Theodore R. Sizer, *Horace's Compromise: The Dilemma of the American High School* (Boston: Houghton Mifflin, 1984), p. 20.

ules seem to segment, to keep things apart from one another, rather than to create lines that hold them together. The recursive approach, with its regular return to important tasks and emphasis on gradual growth, is one way to have time work for rather than against us. But additional strategies are needed, and their invention and testing will require close collaboration between teachers and school administrators. In this, it is our strong feeling that English teachers must come forward with possible solutions. There is increasing sensitivity to the need and an active willingness to address it. What we want are more ideas, more experiments, and more communication about what works and what does not.

High School–College Collaboration

The importance of time and how we use it is not a matter for the high school years alone. We all know that good education requires sustained attention and effort, beginning very early in a child's life and involving parents, teachers, peers, and community. So far as schooling is concerned, we view the different educational levels and institutions not as discrete and separable compartments, but as parts of a whole educational process. The problem has been to act on this vision in a society as large and complex as our own.

There are as many parts to this problem as there are levels and divisions of the educational process. The Green Book and its companion books attend particularly to successful negotiation of the passage between high school and college, and in doing so attempt to clarify the unity of what students need to know and be able to do in order to take good advantage of learning opportunities at both levels. This statement of common ground results from a dialogue among high school and college teachers carried on over the last five years. Within its own scope, it seeks both to reflect and foster the kind of close collegial relations between high schools and colleges urged by James R. Vivian in the following statement.

> There is, in my view, no more important recommendation in the Carnegie Foundation Special Report on *School and College* than the one—contained also in the Carnegie Report on *High School*—that calls for universities and schools to develop genuine partnerships based on the needs of schools as determined by their principals and teachers. Both

aspects of that recommendation are essential: not only that universities and schools work together, but especially that those of us in higher education encourage our colleagues in schools to show us the ways we can marshall our resources to address their needs.[2]

Vivian writes with particular reference to the work of the Yale–New Haven Teachers Institute, an ongoing collaborative project in which secondary school teachers and university faculty join together to prepare curriculum units and pedagogical strategies for use in the New Haven Public Schools (for a full account see *Teaching in America: The Common Ground*).[3] This project and others like it affirm that the problems and missions of school and college are fundamentally intertwined. Colleges have a vested interest in the prior education of their students, and we need greater recognition that college faculties cannot stand aloof, whether they praise or deplore the products of the secondary schools. The fact is that many high school teachers hear from their colleagues in higher education only indirectly and anecdotally, from stories their former students bring about what is said and done in college classrooms. This, obviously, is not enough to maintain clear understanding of the common endeavor.

We need to find ways to create many more working partnerships of college and school faculties that center on the what and how of teaching. Such partnerships are needed at other levels as well—between high school and middle school teachers, as an example. Given different local or regional conditions, such undertakings might take a variety of forms and adopt different practices. Nevertheless, discussion of any joint endeavor of this kind could benefit from consideration of the four principles that have guided the Yale–New Haven effort since its beginning in 1978: (1) a belief in the fundamental importance of the classroom teacher and of teacher-developed materials for effective learning; (2) an insistence that teachers of students at different levels interact as colleagues, addressing common problems of teaching their disciplines; (3) the

---

2. James R. Vivian, in *Teaching in America: The Common Ground* (New York: College Entrance Examination Board, 1985), p. 8.

3. *Teaching in America: The Common Ground* (New York: College Entrance Examination Board, 1985).

conviction that any effort to improve teaching must be "teacher-centered"; (4) a certainty that colleges can assist in improving schools only if they make a significant and long-term commitment to do so.

Writing across the Curriculum

This book and the books about the other basic subjects say a great deal about the importance of "learning across the curriculum"—in this case, about the opportunity and responsibility that teachers in most disciplines have to help students improve their writing. We want to suggest that it is an idea that will continue to demand consideration, regardless of our imperfections or outright failures in incorporating it fully into teaching practice. It will not go away, because it follows from the basic fact that students learn to write through writing, and this is the case wherever and however the writing takes place. So when teachers assign tasks that involve written work they are both adding to and intervening in the student's total, cumulative experience of the writing process.

Basic as this may be, it does not necessarily result in confidence among colleagues in other areas that they know how to assist students with their writing or that they can afford to take the time to do so. In schools where the necessary understandings are not well developed, teachers of English may want to consider some very simple initiatives. For example, it often helps to lead an informal working session on the oft-heard lament, "Students can't write." What does this mean? Collegial consideration of actual examples of student written work drawn from across the curriculum probably will reveal that it means different things and that most teachers can point to what these things are if they are not asked to do so in unfamiliar terminology or with technical precision. Poor spelling, weak vocabulary, lack of organization? In the beginning, it matters less what emerges, or that diagnosis is perfect, than that colleagues begin to feel comfortable with the subject and gain a sense that there is a basis for common action. In the early stages, small steps are more likely to meet with welcome than are highly sophisticated strategies.

In building an approach to writing across the curriculum we may also have to challenge ourselves and become more open to change. It is not only our colleagues in other subject areas who are resistant. Teachers of English also may fear the spotlight or the loss of cherished ground. Some questions we have to ask include the following.

- *Are we willing to take the lead?* The school and our colleagues will look to us for initiatives and guidance. Little will happen unless English teachers set things in motion. How do we prepare ourselves for this responsibility, and how do we acquire the ability to share it with others?
- *Are we open to reciprocity?* Colleagues may argue that we rely too heavily on literature in teaching both writing and reading. Are we prepared to use materials important in other subjects, such as articles on a scientific subject or a political issue?
- *Do we have the necessary commitment?* Full implementation of a strategy for writing across the curriculum takes several years. Can we persevere through the inevitable obstacles and take satisfaction in gradual improvement?

There are now in our schools enough successful approaches to writing across the curriculum to know that there are good reasons to believe that discussions will find positive answers to these and other questions. The gains are great for our students. To have teachers in most classrooms involved in the writing process sharpens alertness to writing problems, builds greater virtuosity into the writing program, and provides more sustained attention to student writing needs. It does not, however, lighten the work load of the English teacher by shifting responsibility elsewhere. What it does is to share understanding of this responsibility and so reduce unhelpful "noise" about student writing performance while increasing the resources we have for improving it.

Questioning

Throughout this book we have placed great importance on the relation between good teaching and asking good questions. Perhaps we may even say that making and using good questions is a basic competency needed for achieving our educational aims. One does not have to be a zealous believer in the Socratic method to know that questions engender thought and tap energies. Moreover, it is our questions that actually shape and give direction to class discussions, tests, projects, and reports—and, we have suggested, to the English curriculum as a whole. It may not be too much to say that good questions are our most effective teaching tools, and most of us could benefit from more practice and preparation in their use.

Earlier, we suggested yet another aspect of the value of good questions. They are the primary means through which we avoid creating a seeming (but false) division between skills and knowledge, competence and content. Good questions engage content and, as they do so, elicit from students the exercise of skills that build academic competence. We want to underline once again the importance of providing this active, challenging experience to all students. Observation suggests that sometimes, even frequently, we do not. Benjamin Bloom reports that:

> Observations of teacher interaction with students in the classroom reveal that teachers frequently direct their teaching and explanation to some students and ignore others. They give much positive reinforcement and encouragement to some students but not to others, and they encourage active participating in the classroom from some students and discourage it from others. The studies find that typically teachers give students in the top third of the class the greatest attention and students in the bottom third of the class receive the least attention and support.[4]

John Goodlad, in *A Place Called School,* adds further to this picture.

> . . . lower track classes tend to emphasize the mechanical mechanics of English usage, whereas high track classes were likely to stress the intellectual skills of analysis, evaluation, and judgment, especially through literature. The low track classes were unlikely to encounter the high status knowledge dealt with in the upper tracks and normally considered essential for college admission.[5]

---

4. Benjamin Bloom, ed., *Taxonomy of Educational Objectives, Handbook I: Cognitive Domain* (New York: David McKay, 1967), p. 11.

5. John Goodlad, *A Place Called School* (New York: McGraw-Hill, 1984), p. 205.

These findings at once come as no surprise and yet seem not to apply to ourselves. This is not a matter of wanting to avoid judgment so much as it is a consequence of not being able to track ourselves instant by instant in the activity of the classroom experience. We fail to notice, perhaps, how often we look to the student who can help things along instead of seeking out the student who most needs our help.

We need to find ways to overcome this situation. Students regarded as low achievers deserve not only full support and encouragement but also the same opportunity to deal with imaginative, challenging questions as their high-achieving counterparts receive. If students in difficulty are excused from responding to questions, they are, in consequence, denied our most effective teaching. We must therefore find ways to look at our own teaching from the dual perspective of equity and quality. Here are some possibilities to consider. We can reflect on and analyze the questions that we ask different students. Is it the case that we direct our most interesting and significant questions to students who we anticipate will give a higher order of response? If we cannot be sure, there are other measures to consider.

- Arrange for a videotaping of our classes and analyze our teaching from the point of view of equitable interaction with all students. If technical assistance is not available, ask a trusted and experienced colleague to observe and provide feedback.

- Establish goals for involvement of specific students. We can, for example, preselect four or five students to whom we will, over several days, ask two or three questions designed to challenge and elicit significant responses.

- Maintain patience in building student competence through questioning. Students who have rarely been asked challenging questions will probably have little skill or interest in answering them: they and we can easily become discouraged. We must remember that competence comes slowly and that silence seldom means that nothing is happening. Experience indicates that the determination to ask is finally repaid by an equal determination to answer.

- Seek to have students frame and ask their own questions. If students rely entirely on questions asked by teachers, they will remain dependent learners. The ultimate purpose of the teacher is to encourage students to become independent learners. Students become independent—and thus responsible—to the extent that they formulate significant questions for which they desire to have answers.

Teachers as Learners

Finally, we want to suggest exploration of a point made again and again in many studies. The great resource of our schools is their teachers. Perhaps the thing most needed for the care and nurture of this resource is the provision for teachers to remain learners. Recently, James Vivian has recalled that many of the most influential analysts of our schools in the past century have emphasized the importance of the continuing intellectual engagement of teachers with the subject they teach.

> In a series of widely read essays published in 1892, Joseph M. Rice argued that "teachers must constantly endeavor to grow both in professional and in general intellectual strength." Having observed schools in 36 cities, Rice concluded, "by far the most progress has been made in those cities where the teachers themselves are the most earnest students. . . . [It is], after all, the teacher that makes the school." The Carnegie Report of 1920 on *The Professional Preparation of Teachers* spoke of the importance of "regular periods of uninterrupted study" for teachers because "the present vitality of the school is directly involved. . . ." In 1963 James B. Conant's *The Education of American Teachers* recommended especially continuing study and in-service education for teachers. Most recently, in the Carnegie Report on *High School* Ernest L. Boyer called for greater emphasis on subject matter in the initial preparation of the teacher and for "a planned continuing education program . . . [as] part of every teacher's professional life."[6]

A point so often made might seem to be well established, and yet we think that it bears further discussion and development. We

---

6. James R. Vivian, in *Teaching in America: The Common Ground* (New York: College Entrance Examination Board, 1985), pp. xxii-xiv.

believe ways must be found for teachers of English to have good, viable opportunities to continue their own intellectual growth—and particularly that they must have the chance to do this through close contact with college faculty.[7] It is urgent that we devise such opportunities to work with our colleagues and to enter into dialogue with them about critical issues. We need to deepen our own art and skill, and, equally important, we need to continue learning in order to remain sensitive to the feelings that are part of the life of the mind—the labor and pleasure, the difficulty and satisfaction, the uncertainty and joy. It is through absorption in our own subject that we keep our vitality and fully grasp what we intend when we ask students to achieve the outcomes we have set for them.

---

7. In connection with this issue, we want to make special note of the importance of reading in both in-service training and continuing education efforts. Recently, we have gained a great deal from our determination to develop and share new approaches to the teaching of writing. We need to apply ourselves in the same way to the teaching of literature and to keeping abreast of emerging critical theories. Teachers will find some interesting suggestions and perhaps a place to begin in R. Baird Sherman's "Keeping Current in Critical Theory" (*English Journal*, October 1984, pp. 59-63).

Bibliography

In a small book it is possible to mention only a few of the resources available to English teachers who want to think further about the issues currently before the profession. We make note particularly of the professional organizations that publish journals, monographs, and books related directly to the teaching of English in the secondary schools and that sponsor national and regional conferences. The National Council of Teachers of English (NCTE) publishes both the *English Journal* and *College English,* two publications that generally contain articles of interest to high school English teachers. Two of its other publications, less well known to secondary teachers of English, *Elementary English* and *Research in the Teaching of English,* are also important. The latter is of particular value in keeping current with research studies and their implications for pedagogy. Finally, NCTE is also the source for the publication *College Composition and Communication,* a journal containing articles of interest to high school teachers of English. There are numerous state and regional associations of English teachers as well; most publish journals and hold conferences.

Other organizations, including the Modern Language Association, the Association for Supervision and Curriculum Development, the National Association of Secondary School Principals, and the College Board, publish journals or occasional pieces relating directly to the teaching of English. In addition, articles in journals and other publications from the American Educational Research Association often contain reports of relevant studies. All these sources should be available to English teachers on request.

In addition, the American Association for Higher Education has published *Writing across the Curriculum* (1984), a monograph that contains both specific articles directed to the purpose explicit in the title and an annotated bibliography about writing. ERIC (Educational Resources Information Center) has developed *Especially for Teachers: ERIC Documents for the Teaching of Writing, 1966-1981.* This publication contains briefly annotated references to a vast range of articles and monographs listed according to subjects such as "Pre-writing Stage" and "Varying the Audience." It is a very useful publication to have and can save teachers time in seeking out relevant and timely materials.

A few of the many other works that may be helpful are listed below.

Articles

Bloom, Benjamin S. "The 2 Sigma Problem: The Search for Methods of Group Instruction as Effective as One-to-One Teaching." *Educational Researcher* 13, no. 6 (June-July 1984): 4-16.

Burton, Dwight. "Literature Today: An Attempt to Be Objective." *English Journal* 69, no. 5 (May 1980): 30-33.

Calabrese, Marilyn. "I Don't Grade Papers Anymore." *English Journal* 71, no. 1 (January 1982): 28-31.

Collins, James L. "Dialect Variation and Writing: One Problem at a Time." *English Journal* 68, no. 8 (November 1979): 48-51.

Criscula, Nicholas. "Upgrading Secondary Reading Programs: An Annotated Bibliography." *English Journal* 68, no. 1 (January 1979): 62-66.

Dillon, David. "Does the School Have a Right to Its Own Language?" *English Journal* 69, no. 4 (April 1980): 13-17.

Ede, Lisa, and Andrea Lunsfor. "Audience Addressed/Audience Invoked: The Role of Audience in Composition Theory and Pedagogy." *College Composition and Communication* 35, no. 2 (May 1984): 140-154.

Evans, Ronald. "The Question about Literature." *English Journal* 71, no. 2 (February 1982): 57-60.

Fahnstock, Jeanne, and Marie Secor. "Teaching Argument: A Theory of Types." *College Composition and Communication* 34, no. 1 (February 1983): 20-30.

Ferguson, Anna Marie. "A Case for Teaching Standard English to Black Students." *English Journal* 72, no. 3 (March 1982): 82-84.

Finch, Gary A., et al. "Teaching Composition in an Urban High School." *English Journal* 68, no. 8 (November 1979): 43-47.

Flanigan, Michael C. "Composition Models: Dynamic and Static Imitations." *Theory into Practice* XIX, no. 3 (Summer 1980): 211-219.

Flower, Linda, and John R. Hayes. "A Cognitive Process Theory of Writing." *College Composition and Communication* 32, no. 4 (December 1981): 365-387.

Franza, August. "How to Read an Ad." *English Journal* 72, no. 6 (October 1983): 32-39.

Fulwiler, Toby. "How Well Does Writing across the Curriculum Work?" *College English* 46, no. 2 (February 1984): 112-125.

Harwood, John. "Focus: English for Everyone: The Teaching of English,

Social Mobility, and the Ideology of Merit." *English Journal* 69, no. 4 (April 1981): 30-37.

Haynes, Elizabeth F. "Using Research in Preparing to Teach Writing." *English Journal* 67, no. 1 (January 1978): 82-88.

Hollowell, John. "Bait: We Should Abolish the Use of Personal Journals in English Classes." *English Journal* 71, no. 1 (January 1982): 14-16.

Horner, Judith. "How Do We Know How Well Kids Write?" *English Journal* 67, no. 7 (October 1978): 60-61

Jacobs, Suzanne. "Composing the In-Class Essay: A Case Study of Rudy." *College English* 46, no. 1 (January 1984): 34-42.

Knoll, Barry. "Writing for Readers: Three Perspectives on Audience." *College Composition and Communication* 35, no. 2 (May 1984): 155-171.

Levenson, Stanley. "Teaching Reading and Writing to Limited and Non-English Speakers in Secondary Schools." *English Journal* 68, no. 8 (November 1979): 38-42

Miller, Robert K. "The Use of Literature in English Composition." *English Journal* 69, no. 9 (December 1980): 54-55.

Moore, Michael. "Writing to Learn, Writing to Teach." *English Journal* 72, no. 5 (September 1983): 34.

Moran, Charles. "Word Processing and the Teaching of Writing." *English Journal* 72, no. 2 (February 1983): 105-108.

Mortimer, Howard. "To Teach Them to Write-Write." *English Journal* 65, no. 6 (September 1976): 57-58.

Murray, Donald M. "Writing and Teaching for Surprise." *College English* 46, no. 1 (January 1984): 1-7.

Petrosky, Anthony R., and James R. Brozick. "A Model for Teaching Writing Based upon Current Knowledge of the Composing Process." *English Journal* 68, no. 1 (January 1979): 96-101.

Purves, Alan. "The State of Research in Teaching Literature." *English Journal* 70, no. 3 (March 1981): 82-84.

Reed, Daisy F. "Helping Black Students Speak Standard English." *English Journal* 72, no. 2 (February 1983): 105-108.

Sampson, G. P., and Nancy Carlman. "A Hierarchy of Student Responses to Literature." *English Journal* 71, no. 1 (January 1982): 54.

Sherman, R. Baird. "Keeping Current in Critical Theory." *English Journal* 73, no. 7 (October 1984): 59-63.

Streznewski, Marylou K. "The Case for Teaching All the Students." *English Journal* 68, no. 2 (February 1979): 24-27.

Turner, Darwin T. "The Teaching of Literature by Afro-Americans," in *The Promise of English: NCTE 1970 Distinguished Lecture Series*. Urbana, Illinois: National Council of Teachers of English, 1970.

Walsh, R. D. "What's Basic to Teaching Writing?" *English Journal* 68, no. 9 (December 1979): 51-56.

Withey, Margaret. "The Computer and Writing." *English Journal* 72, no. 7 (November 1983): 24-32.

Books

Applebee, Arthur N. *Writing in the Secondary School: English and the Content Areas*, NCTE Research Report No. 21. Urbana, Illinois: National Council of Teachers of English, 1981.
————. *Tradition and Reform in the Teaching of English: A History.* Urbana, Illinois: National Council of Teachers of English, 1974.
Association for Supervision and Curriculum Development. *ASCD Curriculum Update.* Alexandria, Virginia: ASCD, April 1984.
Bloom, Benjamin S. (ed.). *Taxonomy of Educational Objectives, Handbook I: Cognitive Domain.* New York: David McKay, 1967.
Boyer, Ernest. *High School: A Report on Secondary Education in America.* New York: Harper & Row, 1983.
Britton, James, et al. *The Development of Writing Abilities.* London: Macmillan Education, 1975.
Coe, Richard. *Form and Substance.* New York: John Wiley and Sons, 1981.
College Entrance Examination Board. *End-of-Year Examinations in English for College-Bound Students, Grades 9-12.* Princeton, New Jersey: College Entrance Examination Board, 1963.
————. *Teaching in America: The Common Ground.* New York: College Entrance Examination Board, 1985.
Diedrich, Paul B. *Measuring Growth in English.* Urbana, Illinois: National Council of Teachers of English, 1974.
Dixon, John. *Growth through English.* London: National Association of the Teaching of English, 1967.
Duke, Charles R. (ed.). *Writing Exercises from Exercise Exchange*, Vol. II. Urbana, Illinois: National Council of Teachers of English, 1984.
Egan, Kieran. *Educational Development.* New York: Oxford University Press, 1979.
Elbow, Peter. *Writing without Tea.* London: Oxford University Press, 1973.
Emig, Janet. *The Composing Process of Twelfth Graders.* Urbana, Illinois: National Council of Teachers of English, 1971.
Farrell, Edmund J. *Deciding the Future: A Forecast of Responsibilities of Secondary Teachers of English, 1970-2000 AD.* Urbana, Illinois: National Council of Teachers of English, 1971.
Glatthorn, Allan A. *A Guide for Developing an English Curriculum in the Eighties.* Urbana, Illinois: National Council of Teachers of English, 1980.

Goodlad, John. *A Place Called School.* New York: McGraw-Hill, 1984.

Harmin, Merrill, Sidney Simon, and Howard Kirschenbaum. *Clarifying Values through Subject Matter: Applications for the Classroom.* Minneapolis, Minnesota: Winston Press, 1973.

Hirsch, E.D. *The Philosophy of Composition.* Chicago: University of Chicago Press, 1981.

Holbrook, David. *English for Maturity.* New York: Cambridge University Press, 1961.

Horton, Susan. *Thinking Through Writing.* Baltimore, Maryland: Johns Hopkins University Press, 1982.

Irmsher, William F. *Teaching Expository Writing.* New York: Holt, Rinehart & Winston, 1979.

Judy, Stephen. *Explorations in the Teaching of English.* New York: Harper & Row, 1981.

Mandel, Barrett J. (ed.). *Three Language Arts Curriculum Models: Pre-Kindergarten through College.* Urbana, Illinois: National Council of Teachers of English, 1980.

Moffett, James. *Active Voice.* Montclair, New Jersey: Boynton/Cook, 1981.

Moffett, James, and Betty Jane Wagner. *Student-Centered Language Arts and Reading, K-13: A Handbook for Teachers*, 2nd ed. Boston: Houghton Mifflin, 1976.

Murphy, Geraldine. *The Study of Literature in High School.* Waltham, Massachusetts: Blaisdell Publishing, 1968.

Myers, John W. *Writing to Learn across the Curriculum.* Bloomington, Indiana: Phi Delta Kappa Educational Foundation, 1984.

National Council of Teachers of English, *Classroom Practices in Teaching English, 1979-80: How to Handle the Paper Load.* Urbana, Illinois: NCTE, 1981.

———. *Documents on the Teaching of Writing.* Urbana, Illinois: ERIC Documents on the Teaching of Writing, 1966-1981. NCTE, 1981.

———. *Especially for Teachers.* Urbana, Illinois: *ERIC Documents for the Teaching of Writing, 1966-1981.* NCTE, 1982.

———. *Idea Exchange for English Teachers.* Urbana, Illinois: NCTE, 1983.

Nelson-Herber, Joan, and Harold L. Herber. "A Positive Approach to Assessment and Correction of Reading Difficulties in Middle and Secondary Schools," in James Flood, ed., *Promoting Reading Comprehension.* Newark, Delaware: International Reading Association, 1984.

Richards, I.A. *Practical Criticism.* New York: Harcourt Brace, 1929.

Rosenblatt, Louise. *The Reader, the Text, the Poem.* Carbondale, Illinois: Southern Illinois University Press, 1978.

Sanders, Norris M. *Classroom Questions, What Kinds?* New York: Harper & Row, 1966.

Shaughnessy, Mina. *Errors and Expectations.* New York: Oxford University Press, 1977.

Sizer, Theodore R. *Horace's Compromise: The Dilemma of the American High School.* Boston: Houghton Mifflin, 1984.

Squire, James R., and Roger K. Applebee. *A Study of English Programs in Selected High Schools which Consistently Educate Outstanding Students in English,* Cooperative Research Project No. 19994. Urbana, Illinois: University of Illinois, 1968.

Stone, George Winchester, Jr. (ed.). *Issues, Problems, and Approaches in the Teaching of English.* New York: Holt, Rinehart & Winston, 1961.

Thaiss, Christopher. *Writing to Learn: Essays and Reflections on Writing across the Curriculum.* Dubuque, Iowa: Kendall/Hunt Publishing Co., 1983.

Weathers, Winston. *An Alternate Style.* Rochelle Park, New Jersey: Hayden, 1980.

Weigand, James E. (ed.). *Developing Teacher Competencies.* Englewood Cliffs, New Jersey: Prentice-Hall, Inc., 1971.

Whitehead, Frank. *The Disappearing Dais.* London: Chatto & Windus, Ltd., 1966.

Wiener, Harvey S. *The Writing Room.* New York: Oxford University Press, 1981.

Appendix A

Excerpt from *A Walker in the City,* by Alfred Kazin.[1]

In Brownsville tenements the kitchen is always the largest room and the center of the household. As a child I felt that we lived in a kitchen to which four other rooms were annexed. My mother, a "home" dressmaker, had her workshop in the kitchen. She told me once that she had begun dressmaking in Poland at thirteen; as far back as I can remember, she was always making dresses for the local women. She had an innate sense of design, a quick eye for all the subtleties in the latest fashions, even when she despised them, and great boldness. For three or four dollars she would study the fashion magazines with a customer, go with the customer to the remnants store on Belmont Avenue to pick out the material, argue the owner down—all remnants stores, for some reason, were supposed to be shady, as if the owners dealt in stolen goods—and then for days would patiently fit and baste and sew and fit again. Our apartment was always full of women in their housedresses sitting around the kitchen table waiting for a fitting. My little bedroom next to the kitchen was the fitting room. The sewing machine, an old nut-brown Singer with golden scrolls painted along the black arm and engraved along the two tiers of little drawers massed with needles and thread on each side of the treadle, stood next to the window and the great coal-black stove which up to my last year in college was our main source of heat. By December the two outer bedrooms were closed off, and used to chill bottles of milk and cream, cold borscht and jellied calves' feet.

The kitchen held our lives together. My mother worked in it all day long, we ate in it almost all meals except the Passover *seder,* I did my homework and first writing at the kitchen table, and in winter I often had a bed made up for me on three kitchen chairs near the stove. On the wall just over the table hung a long horizontal mirror that sloped to a ship's prow at each end and was lined in cherry wood. It took up the whole wall, and drew every object in the kitchen to itself. The walls were fiercely stippled whitewash, so often rewhitened by my father in slack seasons that the paint looked as if it had been squeezed and cracked into the

1. Alfred Kazin, "The Kitchen," in *A Walker in the City* (New York and London: Harcourt Brace Jovanovich, 1951), pp. 64-71.

walls. A large electric bulb hung down the center of the kitchen at the end of a chain that had been hooked into the ceiling; the old gas ring and key still jutted out of the wall like antlers. In the corner next to the toilet was the sink at which we washed, and the square tub in which my mother did our clothes. Above it, tacked to the shelf on which were pleasantly ranged square, blue-bordered white sugar and spice jars, hung calendars from the Public National Bank on Pitkin Avenue and the Minsker Progressive Branch of the Workman's Circle; receipts for the payment of insurance premiums, and household bills on a spindle; two little boxes engraved with Hebrew letters. One of these was for the poor, the other to buy back the Land of Israel. Each spring a bearded little man would suddenly appear in our kitchen, salute us with a hurried Hebrew blessing, empty the boxes (sometimes with a sidelong look of disdain if they were not full), hurriedly bless us again for remembering our less fortunate Jewish brothers and sisters, and so take his departure until the next spring, after vainly trying to persuade my mother to take still another box. We did occasionally remember to drop coins in the boxes, but this was usually only on the dreaded morning of "midterms" and final examinations, because my mother thought it would bring me luck. She was extremely superstitious, but embarrassed about it, and always laughed at herself whenever, on the morning of an examination, she counseled me to leave the house on my right foot. "I know it's silly," her smile seemed to say, "but what harm can it do? It may calm God down."

The kitchen gave special character to our lives; my mother's character. All my memories of that kitchen are dominated by the nearness of my mother sitting all day long at her sewing machine, by the clacking of the treadle against the linoleum floor, by the patient twist of her right shoulder as she automatically pushed at the wheel with one hand or lifted the foot to free the needle where it had got stuck in a thick piece of material. The kitchen was her life. Year by year, as I began to take in her fantastic capacity for labor and her anxious zeal, I realized it was ourselves she kept stitched together. I can never remember a time when she was not working. She worked because the law of her life was work, work and anxiety; she worked because she would have found life meaningless without work. She read almost no English; she could read the Yiddish paper, but never felt she had time to. We were always talking of a time when I would teach her how to read, but somehow there was never time. When I awoke in the morning she was already at her machine, or in the great morning crowd of housewives at the grocery getting fresh rolls for breakfast. When I returned from school she was at her machine, or conferring over *McCall's* with some neighborhood woman who had come in pointing hopefully to an illustration—"Mrs. Kazin! Mrs. Kazin! Make me a dress like it shows here in the picture!" When my father came home from work she had somehow mysteriously interrupted herself to make supper for us, and the dishes cleared and washed, was back at her machine. When I went to bed at night, often she was still there, pounding away at the treadle, hunched over the wheel, her hands steering a piece of gauze under the needle with finesse that always contrasted sharply with her swollen hands and broken nails. Her left hand had been pierced through when as a girl she had worked in the infamous Triangle Shirtwaist Factory on the East Side. A needle had gone straight through the palm, severing a large vein. They had sewn it up for her so clumsily that a tuft of flesh always lay folded over the palm.

The kitchen was the great machine that set our lives running; it whirred down a little only on Saturdays and holy days. From my mother's kitchen I gained my first picture of life as a white, overheated, and starkly lit workshop redolent with Jewish cooking, crowded with women in house-dresses, strewn with fashion magazines, patterns, dress material, spools of thread—and at whose center, so lashed to her machine that bolts of energy seemed to dance out of her hands and feet as she worked, my mother stamped the treadle hard against the floor, hard, hard, and silently, grimly at war, beat out the first rhythm of the world for me.

Every sound from the street roared and trembled at our windows—a mother feeding her child on the doorstep, the screech of the trolley cars on Rockaway Avenue, the eternal smash of a handball against the wall of our house, the clatter of *"der Italyener"*'s cart packed with watermelons, the sing-song of the old-clothes men walking Chester Street, the cries *"Arbes! Arbes! Kinder! Kinder! Heyse gute arbes!"* All day long people streamed into our apartment as a matter of course—"customers," upstairs neighbors, downstairs neighbors, women who would stop in for a half-hour's talk, salesmen, relatives, insurance agents. Usually they came in without ringing the bell—everyone knew my mother was always at home. I would hear the front door opening, the wind whistling through our front hall, and then some familiar face would appear in our kitchen with the same bland, matter-of-fact inquiring look: no need to stand on ceremony: my mother and her kitchen were available to everyone all day long.

At night the kitchen contracted around the blaze of light on the cloth, the patterns, the ironing board where the iron had burned a black border around the tear in the muslin cover; the finished dresses looked so frilly as they jostled on their wire hangers after all the work my mother had put into them. And then I would get that strangely ominous smell of tension from the dress fabrics and the burn in the cover of the ironing board—as if each piece of cloth and paper crushed with light under the naked bulb might suddenly go up in flames. Whenever I pass some small tailoring shop still lit up at night and see the owner hunched over his steam press; whenever in some poorer neighborhood of the city I see through a window some small crowded kitchen naked under the harsh light glittering in the ceiling, I still smell that fiery breath, that warning of imminent fire. I was always holding my breath. What I must have felt most about ourselves, I see now, was that we ourselves were like kindling—that all the hard-pressed pieces of ourselves and all the hard-used objects in that kitchen were like so many slivers of wood that might go up in flames if we came too near the white-blazing filaments in that naked bulb. Our tension itself was fire, we ourselves were forever burning—to live, to get down the foreboding in our souls, to make good.

Twice a year, on the anniversaries of her parents' deaths, my mother placed on top of the ice-box an ordinary kitchen glass packed with wax, the *yortsayt*, and lit the candle in it. Sitting at the kitchen table over my homework, I would look across the threshold to that mourning-glass, and sense that for my mother the distance from our kitchen to *der heym*, from life to death, was only a flame's length away. Poor as we were, it was not poverty that drove my mother so hard; it was loneliness—some endless bitter brooding over all those left behind, dead or dying or soon to die; a loneliness locked up in her kitchen that dwelt every day on the hazardousness of life and the nearness of death, but still kept struggling in the lock, trying to get us through by endless labor.

With us, life started up again only on the last shore. There seemed to be no middle ground between despair and the fury of our ambition. Whenever my mother spoke of her hopes for us, it was with such unbelievingness that the likes of us would ever come to anything, such abashed hope and readiness for pain, that I finally came to see in the flame burning on top of the ice-box death itself burning away the bones of poor Jews, burning out in us everything but courage, the blind resolution to live. In the light of that mourning-candle, there were ranged around me how many dead and dying—how many eras of pain, of exile, of dispersion, of cringing before the powers of this world!

It was always at dusk that my mother's loneliness came home most to me. Painfully alert to every shift in the light at her window, she would suddenly confess her fatigue by removing her pince-nez, and then wearily pushing aside the great mound of fabrics on her machine, would stare at the street as if to warm herself in the last of the sun. "How sad it is!" I once heard her say. "It grips me! It grips me!" Twilight was the bottommost part of the day, the chillest and loneliest time for her. Always so near to her moods, I knew she was fighting some deep inner dread, struggling against the returning tide of darkness along the streets that invariably assailed her heart with the same foreboding— Where? Where now? Where is the day taking us now?

Yet one good look at the street would revive her. I see her now, perched against the windowsill, with her face against the glass, her eyes almost asleep in enjoyment, just as she starts up with the guilty cry—"What foolishness is this in me!"—and goes to the stove to prepare supper for us: a moment, only a moment, watching the evening crowd of women gathering at the grocery for fresh bread and milk. But between my mother's pent-up face at the window and the winter sun dying in the fabrics— "Alfred, see how beautiful!"—she has drawn for me one single line of sentience.

Members of the Council on Academic Affairs, 1983-85

Peter N. Stearns, Heinz Professor of History, Carnegie-Mellon University, Pittsburgh, Pennsylvania (*Chair* 1983-85)

Dorothy S. Strong, Director of Mathematics, Chicago Public Schools, Illinois (*Vice Chair* 1983-85)

Victoria A. Arroyo, College Board Student Representative, Emory University, Atlanta, Georgia (1983-84)

Ida S. Baker, Principal, Cape Coral High School, Florida (1984-85)

Michael Anthony Brown, College Board Student Representative, University of Texas, Austin (1983-85)

Jean-Pierre Cauvin, Associate Professor of French, Department of French and Italian, University of Texas, Austin (1983-84)

Alice C. Cox, Assistant Vice President, Student Academic Services, Office of the President, University of California (1983-84, Trustee Liaison 1984-85)

Charles M. Dorn, Professor of Art and Design, Department of Creative Arts, Purdue University, West Lafayette, Indiana (1983-84)

Sidney H. Estes, Assistant Superintendent, Instructional Planning and Development, Atlanta Public Schools, Georgia (1983-85)

David B. Greene, Chairman, Division of Humanities, Wabash College, Crawfordsville, Indiana (1984-85)

Jan A. Guffin, Chairman, Department of English, North Central High School, Indianapolis, Indiana (1983-85)

John W. Kenelly, Professor of Mathematical Sciences, Clemson University, South Carolina (1983-85)

Mary E. Kesler, Assistant Headmistress, The Hockaday School, Dallas, Texas (Trustee Liaison 1983-85)

Arthur E. Levine, President, Bradford College, Massachusetts (1983-85)

Deirdre A. Ling, Vice Chancellor for University Relations and Development, University of Massachusetts, Amherst (Trustee Liaison 1983-84)

Judith A. Lozano-Loredo, Superintendent, Southside Independent School District, San Antonio, Texas (1983-84)

Eleanor M. McMahon, Commissioner of Higher Education, Rhode Island Office of Higher Education, Providence (1984-85)

Jacqueline Florance Meadows, Instructor of Social Science, North Carolina School of Science and Mathematics, Durham (1983-84)

Michael J. Mendelsohn, Professor of English, University of Tampa, Florida (1983-84)

Fay D. Metcalf, History Coordinator/Teacher, Boulder High School, Colorado (1983-85)

Vivian Rivera, College Board Student Representative, Adlai E. Stevenson High School, Bronx, New York (1984-85)

Raul S. Rodriguez, Chair, Language Department, Xaverian High School, Brooklyn, New York (1984-85)

Michael A. Saltman, Chairman, Science Department, Bronxville School, New York (1983-85)

Vivian H. T. Tom, Social Studies Teacher, Lincoln High School, Yonkers, New York (Trustee Liaison 1983-84)

Kenneth S. Washington, Vice Chancellor for Educational Services, Los Angeles Community College District, California (1983-85)

Henrietta V. Whiteman, Director/Professor, Native American Studies, University of Montana, Missoula (1984-85)

Roberto Zamora, Deputy Executive Director, Region One Education Service Center, Edinburg, Texas (1984-85)